JERUSALEM DIARIES
In Tense Times

JERUSALEM DIARIES
In Tense Times

Judy Lash Balint

UPDATED EDITION

gefen
publishing house בית הוצאה לאור
JERUSALEM ◆ NEW YORK

Typesetting: Marzel A.S. – Jerusalem
Cover Design: S. Kim Glassman

3 5 7 9 8 6 4 2

Gefen Publishing House
POB 36004, Jerusalem 91360, Israel
972-2-538-0247 • orders@gefenpublishing.com

Gefen Books
12 New Street Hewlett, NY 11557, USA
516-295-2805 • gefenbooks@compuserve.com

www.israelbooks.com

Printed in Israel

Send for our free catalogue

ISBN 965-229-271-0 (alk. paper)

Library of Congress Cataloging-in-Publication Data:
Balint, Judy Lash, 1952-
Jerusalem diaries: in tense times / Judy Lash Balint
1. Arab-Israeli conflict—1993-. 2. Jerusalem. 3. Balint, Judy Lash. I. Title.
DS119.76.B35 2001 • 956.94'42054'092—dc21 [B] • CIP Number: 2001033716

AUTHOR'S NOTE

The chapters in this updated volume of Jerusalem Diaries take the reader through the end of the year 2001 to chronicle the turmoil of fifteen months of life in Israel under the shadow of Arab violence.

To live in Jerusalem is to live center-stage in Jewish history. Events unfold at an incredible pace, and there's no such thing as just standing by. All of us who claim the privilege of dwelling in the capital of the Jewish people in the 21st century find ourselves playing a role in the maelstrom of Israeli life.

I must say here that I don't claim to be an objective reporter. My observations are colored by the fact that I am a committed Zionist who chooses to live in the Jewish state. Throughout my years here, I have used my press card to travel to places and talk to people infrequently visited by mainstream reporters. Letters make up this volume, which I hope will enrich the reader's understanding of the complexities of Israel's existence.

I have been guided and aided in this effort by several extraordinary people; Rabbi Avi Weiss, my mentor and teacher, whose love of the people, Torah and land of Israel knows no bounds; Chaim Silberstein of Beit Orot, a colleague, friend and role model, whose limitless energy and commitment to Jerusalem are an inspiration; Tova Reich, a brilliant author and friend whose advice and counsel I treasure; Edward Alexander, esteemed professor and comrade-in-arms, and Manfred Vanson, visionary and activist who helped shape my political and Zionist views.

❖   ❖   ❖

Check the Jerusalem Diaries website at **www.jerusalemdiaries.com**
for regular updates from Judy in Jerusalem

Special thanks to Eli and Rebecca Almo, Michael and Elana Fischberger, Gigi and Wolf Kohn, Jeff and Hillary Markowitz, Morey and Barbara Schapira and Ronn Torrossian for their friendship, encouragement and support for this project.

❖   ❖   ❖

This book is dedicated to the memory of my dear parents, Werner and Lottie Lash z"tl, and to their future generation, my children: Benjamin and Ilana Balint.

❖   ❖   ❖

Portions of this book have appeared in the New York Post; Jerusalem Post; Jerusalem Report; Forward; Midstream; Jewish Action; Moment; Christian Science Monitor; Seattle Times; Los Angeles Jewish Journal; Arizona Jewish Post; Seattle Jewish Transcript; New Orleans Jewish News.

Photos: Judy Lash Balint, David Cohen, Henry Gerber, Robert Kalfus, Arnold Stark

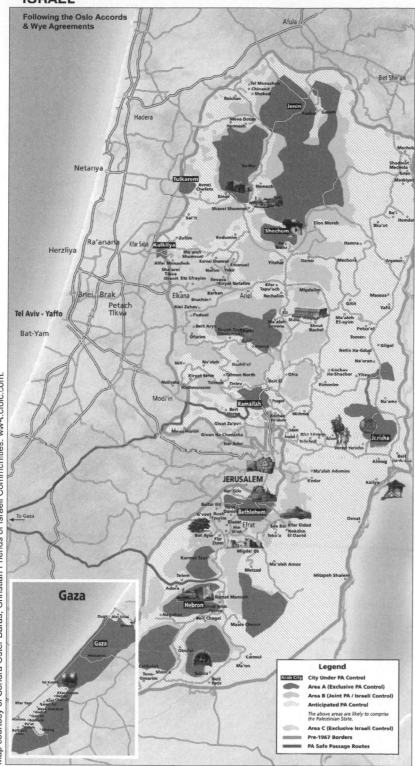

ISRAEL

Following the Oslo Accords
& Wye Agreements

Afula

Bet She'an

Hadera

Netanya

Tal Menasheh
Chinanit
Shaked
Reichan

Jenin
Kadim Ganim

Mechola

Mevo Dotan
Hermesh

Shadmot
Mechola
Rotem
Maskiyot

So-Nura

Ro'i Hemdat

Tulkarem
Avnei
Chefetz
Einav
Homesh

Elon Moreh

Bka'ot

Shavei Shomron

Shechem

Nur Bracha

Ra'anana
Herzliya
Kfar Saba Kalkilya
Zufim
Kedumim

Hamra

Ma'aleh
Shomron
Alfei Menasheh
Sha'arei
Tikva
Dranit Etz Efrayim
Kirvat Netafim
Karnei Shomron
Nofim
Yakir
Emanuel

Yitzhar
Itamar
Mechora

Arganan

Bnei Brak
Tel Aviv - Yaffo
Petach
Tikva
Bat-Yam

Elkana
Bruchin
Alei Zahav
Peduel
Ofarim
Beit Arye
Barkan
Ariel

Revava

Kfar
Tapu'ach
Rechalim
Migdalim

Gitit

Massua
Yafit

El

Ma'aleh
Levona
Shilo
Shvut
Rachel

Ma'aleh
Efrayim
Petza'el
Tomer

Gilgal

Novev Tzuf
(Chalamish)
Ateret

Netiv Ha-Gdud
Na'aran

Nili
Na'aleh
Nachli'el

Kochav
Ha-Shachar
Yitav

Matityahu
Kiryat Sefer
Hashmonaim
Talmon North
Talmon Dolev
Beit El
Ofra

Rimonim

Na'ama

Modi'in
Ramallah
Beit
Horon
Pisgat

Kochav
Ya'akov
Michmas

Jericho

Givat Ze'ev
Givon Ha-Chadasha
Har Adar
Mevo Horon

Alon
Vered Yericho

Beit
Ha-Arava

JERUSALEM

Ma'aleh Adumim

Almog

Kaliya

Har Gilo
Kedar

To Gaza

Beitar Ilit
Neve
Dania Rosh
Tzurim
Elazar
Alon
Sh'vut
Efrat

Bethlehem

Ovnat

G'vaot

Bat Ayin
Kfar
Etzion

Sde Bar Kfar Eldad
Tek'oa Nokdim
El David

Migdal Oz

Karmei Tzur

Ma'aleh Amos
Metzad

Mitzpeh Shalem

Telem
Adora

Ramat Mamreh

Hebron
Kiryat Arba
Hebron
Negohot
Beit Chagai

Maale Chever

Otniel
Carmei

Susiia
Tene- Shim'a
Omarim

Eshkolot
Ma'on

Beit
Yatir

Gaza

Dugit Alei Sinai
Nisanit

Gaza

Netzarim

Tel Katifa
Kfar Darom
Katif
Ganei Tal
Neve
Dekalim
Gadid
Gan Or
Atzmona Bedolach
Pe'at
Rafi'ah Morag
Yam

Contents

Is Real Security at Hand for Israelis?

Jerusalem, November, 1998   Today I'm supposed to feel more secure. My prime minister and the leader of the free world told me so at the White House signing ceremony concluding the Israeli-Palestinian negotiations which took place at Wye Plantation.

Yet as the sun rises on another of the unusually hot, clear days of this autumn in Jerusalem, I feel strangely and uncharacteristically insecure. Not from the "normal" tension that we live with every day in Israel's capital city — the specter of riding the bus into the city early on a Sunday morning — the favored time for Palestinian terror attacks; or knowing that one of my errands would take me to the Ben Yehuda mall, scene of several grisly bombings in recent years — but rather from the turmoil of mixed feelings of disbelief, fear, sadness and resentment brought on by the latest round of concessions wrested from our government.

Disbelief that a Likud government, elected by an overwhelming majority of Jewish voters on a nationalist platform, would act to conclude an agreement which cedes part of our homeland to the Palestine Authority, a body that to this day has not come to terms with Israel's existence and whose frequently declared goal is "a Palestinian state with Jerusalem as its capital."

Disbelief that any Israeli leader would agree to the release of 750 Palestinian terrorists from Israeli jails without obtaining the freedom of one Israeli agent, Jonathan Pollard (indicted on one count of passing classified information to an ally — not of harming the US or its agents), who languishes in a Butner, North Carolina, jail cell for the 14th year of a life sentence.

Fear of the increased security risks inherent in a deal which leaves some 20 small Jewish communities exposed as isolated islands in a sea of armed neighbors. Just imagine feeling safe in Bellevue, Washington, if residents of your neighboring communities of Renton and Kirkland resented your presence there as "settlers"; stockpiled weapons and initiated sporadic terrorist attacks against innocent Bellevue citizens; broadcast children's programming on PBS where kids chant: "When I wander into the entrance of Bellevue I will turn into a suicide warrior in battledress." [Just substitute 'Jerusalem' for 'Bellevue' and you have the February 1998 Palestine Broadcasting Authority Children's Club program].

Sadness that, after fifty years of statehood, Israel still has to justify its existence on land that has belonged to the Jewish people for thousands of years and which we regained in modern times in defensive wars. The Wye Memorandum perpetuates the "land for peace" concept inaugurated at Camp David in 1978 — and we're still waiting for the peace. Never before in history has the idea, that the aggressor should recover whatever territory he lost as a result of his aggression, been sanctioned.

Sadness at the inevitability of armed conflict in the region following the Wye Memorandum. In his 1995 book *A Place Among the Nations*, Benjamin Netanyahu wrote: "It is not difficult to anticipate that the Palestinian organizations, after receiving all that they demand from Israel, will renew with greater vigor terror attacks against Jews, before they declare total war. The significance of ceding land to the PLO is transfer to terrorist forces and Islamic fundamentalists. As a continuation of the implementation of the Oslo Accords, this will cause Israel to be surrounded by a ring of Islamic terror bases which have one goal, and one goal alone: the destruction of the State." He's right — that's why the continuous anti-Jewish violence in Hebron, where large chunks of the city were given over to Palestiniane Authority (PA) control last February, is but a bitter foretaste of what is in store for other communities in Israel if the Wye Memorandum is approved by Bibi's cabinet.

Resentment that the entire Wye agreement is riddled with the subordination of Israeli sovereignty to a US administration with its own agenda. In the five years since the Oslo Accords, the US has never acted on the PA's non-compliance with numerous significant provisions of that agreement. Now the CIA has been entrusted with supervision of the security provisions — the CIA, whose forays into foreign policy territory have been questionable, at best.

And finally, resentment at being labeled "militant," "extremist" or "a religious hard-liner," because I believe that Jews have the right to live in peace anywhere in the Jewish homeland. Or because I view with disbelief, fear and sadness the prospects for real peace in Israel as long as we continue to carve up our land, already significantly smaller than Vancouver Island, in return for the same old assurances of security guarantees and amending charters of hate that Yasser Arafat has promised during every Mideast negotiation.

So, Bill and Bibi, there's a lot more work to be done before I'll feel more secure waking up in Jerusalem tomorrow morning.

Wake Up Call

Jerusalem, November, 1998   The TV images shook every Israeli. Over and over, we see footage of Palestinian "students" from Bir Zeit University shouting "Yahoodi, Yahoodi," (Jew, Jew) as the white car approaches the Ramallah junction just outside the community of Beit El, less than 30 minutes from Jerusalem.

Rocks start flying, the windshield shatters, and dozens of student thugs attack the car, dragging out the passenger, a young IDF soldier, to beat him over the head with large rocks. Clearly visible on the film is one Palestinian grabbing the soldier's M-16 rifle and running off with it. After a few moments, we see the soldier, blood dripping from his head, running away in the direction of a nearby army base. Within minutes, kerosene is poured on the car and all that's left of the confrontation is a charred mass of mangled steel.

Israeli authorities are powerless to go after the perpetrators, even though their faces are clearly identifiable on the video, since the whole incident took place in PA controlled territory.

On this morning's radio talk shows, angry Israelis vent their feelings of fear and impotence. One woman questions why IDF soldiers still carry arms. "I don't blame this soldier," she says, "he was probably afraid of being courtmartialled if he had fired his weapon." Another man, from the coastal town of Bat Yam, sees the sudden explosion of violence, completely unrestrained by either IDF or Palestinian police, and the unmitigated hatred of Jews, as a foretaste of the potential for further outbreaks wherever Israelis and Palestinians exist in close proximity.

An elderly Holocaust survivor calls in to ask how such anti-Semitism could be allowed to occur in the Jewish state. "Jews beaten in the streets just because they're Jews; running away and no one prosecuted! It's an outrage," he declares.

No one mentions the fact that the Ramallah attackers are students — the privileged among Palestinian and Arab society. Israeli students, who are in the sixth week of a strike for reduced tuition, generally are in the forefront of the peace movement. It is completely beyond the imagination to conceive of Israeli students from the Technion or Ben Gurion University going out to the streets looking for Arab victims, yelling "Get the Arab..." Yet the Bir Zeit mob are their counterparts.

So much for President Clinton's remarks at this week's Palestine Donors Conference in Washington, explaining US support for continuing to throw money at the PA. Clinton opined that, "For too long, too many young people have turned to terrorism and old hatreds partly because they had nothing better to do. Every step toward opportunity is a step away from violence." With this misguided view of reality, shouldn't we all be cringing at the legitimacy given to Arafat when the US and PA flags will fly side by side in a few weeks as Clinton addresses the Palestine National Council?

The Ramallah incident almost eclipsed yesterday morning's horrible murder of an Arab sanitation worker in the mixed Arab/Jewish Jerusalem neighborhood of Abu Tor, about four minutes walk from my apartment. The 41-year-old father of six was on his way to work when a masked attacker stabbed him repeatedly, leaving him to die on the sidewalk. Police speculate that one person is responsible for a recent string of knife attacks on Arabs in the capital. Within an hour and a half of the early morning incident, Prime Minister Benjamin Netanyahu and Mayor Ehud Olmert had condemned the attack, calling for harsh prosecution of the assailant.

We're still waiting for any statement on the Ramallah violence from either Arafat or the president of Bir Zeit University. Arab street reaction was swift, however. According to the Jerusalem Post,

---

rocks were thrown at police on the streets of Abu Tor last night, and during the funeral, hundreds of Palestinians clashed with police along Rehov Saleh a-Din, less than half a mile away from Geula and Meah Shearim. Police said that an Israeli Jew driving past the funeral procession was pulled from his car and the vehicle set on fire. This in Israel's capital city — the heart of the Jewish people.

Meantime, the propaganda and real estate battle for Jerusalem is in full swing. As he accepts their millions, Arafat announces to the international community that he won't rest until there's a Palestinian state, with Jerusalem as its capital. Of course most countries of the world, including the US, maintain their embassies in Tel Aviv, not even acknowledging that Jerusalem is the capital of the Jewish state.

Moreover, in violation of the Oslo Accords, the PA operates undisturbed from Orient House, just off one of Jerusalem's main arterial roads. Even a cursory look around the city reveals the extent

Illegal construction and renovation in Silwan
(an Arab residential area across the Kidron Valley from the City of David.)

14

of frenetic illegal Arab building underway. In Abu Dis, the PA already has its capital under construction. Yet two days ago, when building contractors were taken to Har Homa by government officials for a briefing on the terms of a tender, they were met by protestors — not Palestinians, but Peace Now demonstrators, who apparently don't care that Har Homa is strategically placed between PA controlled Bethlehem and Abu Dis to prevent potential attacks of the Ramallah variety on Jewish Jerusalemites.

The past week has also brought the debate over a withdrawal from Lebanon to a crescendo. Seven boys were killed in one week in southern Lebanon. If the IDF can't beat out a few hundred Hizbollah terrorists up there, how are we supposed to believe that they'll be able to repel an onslaught of thousands of armed Palestinians coming at Jewish communities from within a few hundred yards?

So, most of us walk around as in a daze. The situation is on everyone's lips, it colors every conversation and interaction, but no one quite knows how to deal with its reality. Some have taken to stockpiling food and supplies. Almost everyone bemoans the lack of leadership and the corruption inherent in Israeli politics. The reinstatement of David Levy as finance minister is the latest manifestation of that phenomenon.

As we walk through the streets of the city, the sun is shining (still no rain, despite urgent pleas from the rabbinate for increased attention to the prayer for rain), the flowers are in splendid bloom, the birds sing, and kids chatter on their way to kindergarten. Will it look any different when the threat is upon us?

Rachel Still Weeps

Jerusalem, June, 1998   A few days ago a brand new Torah scroll was dedicated for use at one of Judaism's oldest holy places — Kever Rachel, Rachel's Tomb, on the outskirts of Bethlehem.

Kever Rachel has been a place of pilgrimage for Jews for more than 3,000 years. The site is first mentioned in Genesis (35:19-20), where we learn that Rachel was buried "on the road to Efrat, which is Bet Lehem." The famed 12th century Jewish traveler, Benjamin of Tudela, described Kever Rachel in 1170, and until the 19th century nothing changed. Then the tomb was given a domed roof and renovated by Sir Moses Montefiore in 1841. The only period when the tomb was not under Jewish control was the 19 years after it fell into Jordanian hands, from 1948 until the Six Day War in 1967.

But Kever Rachel of 1998 is a very different place from that of even a few years ago. Now an Israeli enclave in PA territory, the domed structure has been covered over and expanded to allow for increased safety for visitors. A five minute journey from the Jewish Jerusalem neighborhoods of Gilo or Talpiot brings you to the concrete barricades protecting Rachel's tomb.

Last Thursday, in a ceremony organized long-distance by Evelyn Haies, a persistent Brooklyn activist, hundreds of people streamed off buses and into the forecourt of Kever Rachel to celebrate the dedication of the new Torah.

The nearby streets had been closed off, and the Israeli army and police maintained a large, high profile presence as the Torah was brought into the compound under a grand chupah, accompanied by an Israeli flag, loud, upbeat Hasidic rock music and scores of dancing men. Inside the kever, hundreds of women packed in to recite Psalms, led by the charismatic Rabbanit Tzipporah Heller, a renowned teacher from Neve Yerushalayim Seminary.

On a platform, rabbinic dignitaries waited their turn to speak in a mixture of English and Hebrew. Several of them, including Rabbi Mayer Horowitz, the son of the Bostoner rebbe, and Rabbi Yehoshua Magnes of Merkaz Harav Kook, alluded to the significance of the prophet Jeremiah's mention of Rachel.

> Rachel is weeping for her children. She refuses to be comforted, because her children are not present. God says, Don't let your voice weep and your eyes fill with tears. For your work will be rewarded, God says, and they shall come back from the land of the enemy. There is hope for the future, and your children will return to their own border. (Jeremiah 31:15-17)

Rabbanit Tzvia Goren, widow of former chief rabbi Shlomo Goren, reminisced about the night in 1967 when she arrived at the kever with her husband and a contingent of IDF soldiers. They entered into the tomb not knowing what they would find after a 19-year absence. She recalled reciting Psalms together with the soldiers, and that the tomb was unadorned by any covering — a situation she quickly rectified.

Rabbi Eliezer Waldman, of the Nir Yeshiva in Kiryat Arba, delivered a powerful message. "The Torah is the Torah of Eretz Yisrael," he said. "The ruach (spirit) of this new Sefer Torah will strengthen and renew our lives." Rabbi Waldman used the opportunity to speak out in support of the beleaguered Arutz-7 radio station, whose offices and studios had been raided by the police the previous week. Then he added: "We're sending a message to our friend, the prime minister. Don't retreat from Jewish land."

Crossing back through the checkpoint I stared back at Palestinian Bet Lehem, and then east toward the vast expanse of Har Homa, where there's still no sign of building activity — maybe it's too soon for Rachel to stop crying.

Stepping Off the Roller Coaster

Negev, November 7, 1998   There's an emotional, roller coaster quality to life in Jerusalem, and it's most evident whenever terrorists choose to disrupt our lives.

When news of the latest Mahane Yehuda bombing came over the radio, I was eighty miles away, driving with friends through the Negev, looking forward to a long planned Shabbat respite at the Sde Boker field school. We listened in stunned silence as the announcer reported two dead and twenty injured. Three thoughts flashed through my mind — I'd been shopping in the market the previous afternoon, I could just as well have been there Friday morning; who amongst my friends might be there, and finally, where was the nearest phone to reassure my family in England and Seattle that I was OK.

The terrorists cast a pall over the Shabbat of every observant Israeli, since it was only at the conclusion of Shabbat we were able to learn that, miraculously, the only fatalities were the two suicide bombers themselves, and that of the injured, only one woman still remained in hospital.

The weekend had started on a much happier note with the Thursday night concert commemorating the fourth yahrzeit of Reb Shlomo Carlebach, the pied piper, roving Hasidic troubadour of Jewish spiritual seekers. The sell-out crowd packed the auditorium at Jerusalem's Binyanei Haooma, the International Conference Center. Bands including Reva L'Sheva, BenZion Solomon and Sons, as well as klezmer genius, Moosa Berlin, played their interpretations of all the old Reb Shlomo favorites, as hundreds, young and old, Israeli and American-born, sang along and danced in the aisles. The four hour marathon also featured video footage of Shlomo connecting with Jews all over the world, as well as a pre-election week appearance by Mayor Ehud OImert.

Negev landscape near Kibbutz Sde Boker.

On Friday morning as we drove south to Sde Boker, some 35 miles south of Beersheva, we played Shlomo tapes until it was time to tune in to the 10:00 a.m. news.

❖　❖　❖

The desert terrain is awesome in its stark beauty, but equally amazing is the man-made development of thriving, lush communities in this inhospitable climate.

Sde Boker was the kibbutz home of David and Paula Ben Gurion. Today, like many kibbutzim, Sde Boker is struggling to retain its membership. The field school where we stayed is adjacent to the burial site of the Ben Gurions and overlooks the spectacular desert canyon of Matzuk Hatzinim, with its fabulous vistas of sandstone formations and majestic hills that change color with the waning daylight. Ibex scamper over the rocks right behind the guest house, and at sunset we could hear the noise of thousands of migratory birds making a rest stop in the bushes toward the bottom of the canyon. Once they had flown on, we just stood there, listening to the silence of the vast desert.

Our visit coincided with the annual Ben Gurion March. Intrepid hikers walk 7-13 kilometers through the Negev, ending up at Sde Boker to pay homage to Ben Gurion. We watched as hundreds of people trekked up the winding road leading to the kibbutz under the relentless mid-day sun. Many families had small kids in tow, and several companies sponsored teams decked out in matching hats and T-shirts. The finish line of the event was in the desert park just behind the Ben Gurion graves. Soft grass and the shade of fragrant eucalyptus trees rewarded the walkers who had spent the past several hours kicking up the dust.

As darkness fell, the soft desert winds picked up. On the way home we stopped the car far away from any source of light and got out to stare up at the night sky. It seemed as if we could see all of the Milky Way and every star flashing its brilliance against the pure black of the sky.

For a few brief moments, it almost felt as if I'd stepped off the roller coaster.

Gas Masks Back in the Closet?

Jerusalem, November 18, 1998   Now that the latest stand-off with Saddam Hussein seems to have been taken off the front burner, we Israelis have to decide whether to put our gas masks away in the back of the closet, or leave them somewhere more accessible for the inevitable next round.

Last Friday, the newspapers here calmly reported that there was only an "extremely remote chance" that Israel would be the target of Saddam Hussein's whims. On the same front page was the announcement that hundreds of gas mask distribution centers were being reopened.

The public was urged to exchange gas masks if they're eight years old — in other words, of Gulf War vintage. Kid's masks are graded according to age, so families must ensure that they have the appropriate size for their offspring. As the TV news showed lines of people at the centers last week, I decided to use some precious free Friday morning hours to get my mask.

On the Internet and in the newspapers, a hotline number in each city was publicized to help find the closest distribution center. A girl doing her national service politely answered the phone after the second ring to patiently explain the location of the center and the closest bus lines.

I made my way to a school in Kiryat Moshe and stepped out of the bright, warm sunshine of a fall Friday into the hustle and bustle of the serious business of protecting the Israeli public. A platoon of reserve duty soldiers — notable by their greying hair and beards — stood fully armed at the gate, while a small group of their colleagues unloaded a truck full of huge boxes marked with the size of the masks they contained.

Notices posted on the school gates in large letters in Hebrew, Russian and English urged the public to obey the instructions of the center commanders and not to give them aggravation since their orders were complete and final. Big signs emphasized that the boxed mask kits are not to opened until the order is given from the Home Command.

In front of me in line was a middle-aged American couple who were still on tourist status despite the fact that they've been here for two months. The wife implored the guard to allocate masks to her and her husband, even though, at present, the kits are only being given to citizens. The Ministry of Tourism has plans to rent masks to tourists via the hotels, should the crisis escalate.

Back in the line, I had a chance to look around at the maelstrom of activity inside. A line of computers covered one wall of the school gym. Huge stacks of boxes were being piled up in the back, and a row of women soldiers manned the desks where the kits were actually distributed. In the foyer, a young soldier was demonstrating how to use the rubber life-savers.

At the computer station, a harried young woman asked for my ID card. Entering my number into the computer she could determine that I had never been issued a mask before. (All official business in Israel is conducted by the teudat zehut — ID card. For better or for worse, the government knows every single office I've been to, every doctor's visit I've made, etc.) After receiving a written OK, she waved me on to the distribution desk. Once again, under the watchful eyes of three or four reserve soldiers standing around with nothing better to do, I produced my blue ID card, signed the receipt and received a bar-coded gas mask kit with a shoulder strap. Handing it over in a plain white nylon bag, she bade me the standard, "Have a nice day," greeting and sent me out to the foyer. I'm sure they'd been given the order to package the masks in bags to avoid hundreds of people wandering around the streets with gas masks slung over their shoulders. The government is clearly trying to avoid the widescale panic which developed during the last Saddam alert in February.

In the hallway, I watched a young couple holding a six month old baby, as they listened intently while the soldier demonstrated and explained the use of the special baby shield. It's a clear plastic contraption which covers the torso and head of the child, and it even has a pouch for a baby bottle! It's hard to visualize any baby lasting more than three minutes in that thing. The parents were shown how to attach the special breathing unit and hook up the straps. Finally, they were given clear instructions on how to use the vial of antidote to nerve gas that comes with a syringe. The father turned to me and said what many of us have been thinking the past few days — this is supposed to make us feel better, but in the event, nothing's going to help.

He picked up his gurgling, cute and oblivious baby daughter, took her kit and walked away with his wife, leaving a small group of adults to the next demonstration. After demonstrating the adult mask, the soldier calmly reminded us of the symptoms to watch for that would necessitate using the anti-nerve gas syringe. Chest pains, body tremors, nausea and vomiting, etc. I was feeling some of these just listening to her! After being handed a small trilingual explanatory brochure, we were ushered out so the next group could receive their instructions.

I walked back to the bus stop through the streets where people were preparing for Shabbat and children were playing. Riding through the center of town, I watched the usual Friday morning cafe life and the banners welcoming a large convention of North American Jews to Israel, fluttering from the lamposts.

The previous Friday morning was the Mahane Yehuda car bomb attack — in this city where so much can happen in a week, it's almost forgotten already. Last Friday was gas mask alert time — would anyone care to predict what we'll be doing next Friday morning, or how long it will be before we unpack those masks again?

Golan Rally Sends Strong Message to Ehud Barak

Tel Aviv, January 1999   There wasn't an inch of breathing space in Kikar Rabin last night, as speaker after speaker emphasized to a passionate crowd that true peace will never come from giving away one of Israel's most strategic assets.

Wire service reports put the number of demonstrators at anywhere between 100,000 (AP) and 200,000 (Reuters). The Jerusalem Post pegged the number at 250,000, while a police officer I spoke to at the scene estimated 300,000 people were there — and organizers claimed more than 400,000.

At Binyanei Haooma in Jerusalem, frantic calls by organizers for more buses were made from cellphones, as it became clear that the number of buses ordered to transport demonstrators to Tel Aviv would be nowhere near sufficient to accommodate the hundreds still waiting in the cold drizzle to get to the rally.

The highway was jammed with buses from all over the country sporting large "Ha'am im Hagolan" (The people are with the Golan) banners. The normal 50-minute journey from Jerusalem to Tel Aviv took more than two hours as the off-ramp into the city became clogged with traffic. Finally, in frustration, the bus drivers opened the doors just off the highway and hundreds poured out to walk the last three quarters of a mile to Kikar Rabin. As we arrived at the packed square, almost two hours after the official start of the program, an announcement was made that the police had closed all entrances to the city for the duration of the rally — hundreds of buses were still waiting outside the closed zone to drop off their passengers. We could see that most of the media had left already, as the cordoned off media area was completely empty.

Those of us who arrived late from other parts of the country missed a screening of a short film about the Golan which featured a closing shot of Yitzhak Rabin in 1992 proclaiming his unalterable opposition to giving away the Golan. (The film may be viewed at the information center in Katzrin.)

Contingents from every part of the country crowded the square and every street leading to it. A group standing in front of me waved a massive banner proclaiming, "Eilat is with the Golan." A full busload of concerned Israelis had driven all afternoon to reach Tel Aviv to stand in solidarity with the Golan.

Organizers were prepared for bad weather — although it stayed dry for most of the three hours of the event. Bright yellow and green umbrellas emblazoned with the Golan slogan were being sold for a small donation, and the pro-Golan stickers that are appearing on an increasing number of Israel's vehicles were stuck to everyone's clothing.

All Israeli political rallies are part politics, part entertainment — necessary to lighten the tension inherent in the heavy decisions we're asked to make. Last night's speeches were interspersed with lively music. One especially popular performer was a Shas-affiliated singer who has put the slogan, "We're not moving from the Golan," to music, with a chorus of "We're staying..."

More than thirty people sat on the speakers' platform (thankfully not all of them addressed the crowd) but they represented a broad cross-section of Israeli political life. This was not the typical "settler" crowd, but a far more diverse section of Israeli society. Not surprising, since a poll taken by the Steinmetz Center of Tel Aviv University revealed that as many as 20 percent of Labor voters may oppose a withdrawal from the Golan, as would a quarter of all Meretz voters. I saw a few signs at the demonstration which read: "I'm a Leftist for the Golan."

Two of the most successful leaders of popular struggles in the history of the nation joined the campaign against withdrawal from the Golan and spoke tonight — Motti Ashkenazi, who led the protest movement after the Yom Kippur War, and Avi Kaddish, a longtime fighter for government reform. Several army reserve generals, as well as Dubi Helman, secretary of the Kibbutz Movement, also addressed the rally.

Lior Katzav, mayor of the development town of Kiryat Mal'achi, spoke of his opposition to the withdrawal and the bill which he predicted would be paid, not by the US, but by Israeli citizens. "If the US Congress had so much trouble approving a few million dollars for the Wye aid bill, why should we think they're going to approve $60 billion for the Golan?" he asked.

Another persuasive speaker was Dmitri Apartziv, the deputy head of the Katzrin Local Council. Apartziv, an immigrant from the former Soviet Union, spoke in Hebrew and Russian, reflecting the large percentage of Russian immigrants in the crowd. Thousands of Jews from the FSU have been resettled in Katzrin, the largest town in the Golan. Apartziv explained that they had been uprooted often enough in their lives, and were not about to go through that experience again for the promise of peace from a terrorist ally of Russia.

One of the most disturbing things about the evening was returning home to watch the TV coverage. Channel 1, Israel TV, did lead off its late night news with footage of the demonstration. The segment was about 15 seconds long, with a voiceover saying there were about 100,000 people there. "But there's other news besides the Golan tonight," the announcer intoned — and we were then treated to a full three minutes about the AOL-Times/Warner merger. CNN Europe, the BBC and SkyNews all included substantial information and pictures from the mass demonstration in their coverage of the wrap-up of the Shepherdstown talks. It seems that Israel TV (subsidized by a tax paid by all Israeli TV owners) is quite content that our European neighbors should be better informed than we, the Israeli voters who will presumably be asked to cast our ballots for the future of the Golan.

As one of the speakers said: "Whatever's in the media tomorrow, each one of you in this massive crowd will go home and to work and tell what really happened here. Remember — you were here on the night we stopped the withdrawal from the Golan."

Winter Time Jerusalem Observations

Jerusalem, February, 1999   With the belated onset of the Jerusalem winter, clear cultural differences emerge among residents of the Holy City. Those from the former Soviet Union stroll about oblivious to the cold, wrapped in the bulky coats, fur lined hats and heavy boots they brought with them from the old country. In contrast, the slight, frail figures of recently arrived Ethiopians stand shivering at the bustops, vainly trying to escape the cold wind by wrapping their white shawls tighter around their shoulders. The Jerusalem Post Fund and an Efrat initiative headed by Rabbanit Vicki Riskin issue urgent appeals for donations of winter shoes for the Ethiopians.

Members of Israel's Defense Forces don't seem to take the winter very seriously. On a recent cold and rainy Sunday morning at the North Tel Aviv bus station, I waited for the bus back to Jerusalem under a dripping shelter, together with platoons of soldiers returning from their Shabbat respite. Only two or three of the youngsters were wearing regulation army jackets — the others were standing around in their regular shirtsleeves as the rain transformed their uniforms with each passing minute from khaki to dark green.

Americans here dress appropriately enough for the weather, but complain about the heat, or lack of heat, in their apartments. Long discussions emerge on the English-speaking immigrant's Internet newslist about how to keep warm. The basic problem is that, since the wintry season is relatively short, and the summer's heat is so intense, buildings here are constructed with summer comfort in mind. Stone floors are the norm. Minimal insulation and windows meant to be opened wide create drafty conditions in most apartments.

Almost every building has a Vaad Bayit — a house committee,

whose job it is to determine at what hours of the day the heat will be turned on. Each apartment owner or renter pays a monthly fee to the Vaad for heat, and usually for general upkeep of the communal stairwell and garden. In my building of six units, the Vaad Bayit charge is 180 shekel ($42) per month, all year. Other Vaads charge more in the winter months and then ease up during the summer. At my place, the powers that be have determined that we don't need heat during the day until 5 pm. Then the radiators are turned on full blast until about midnight; thus, electric space heaters are de rigueur for those who like to get out of bed in the morning without having to put on ten layers of clothing.

Hot water conditions vary from apartment to apartment. I'm lucky — my hot water is linked to the boiler which heats the radiators. So (a) you're guaranteed plenty of hot water at night and first thing in the morning, since the water, unlike the radiators, stays warm all night; and (b) there's no extra bill for electricity to heat the water. In the summer we switch to the solar water heater — another freebie that provides constant hot water.

Some of my fellow immigrants are not so lucky — either they have to pay the electricity bill for their hot water if the tank isn't linked to the heating system, or they don't have any central heating and make do with plug-in radiators, an expensive proposition.

But unlike winter weather in the States, Jerusalem winter days don't seem gray and endless. While we might have a day or two of cold winds and heavy rain, the next few days will be bright and sunny. In the park over Shabbat, kids were playing without coats under blue skies, and many of the sidewalk cafes leave their tables stacked up outside, ready to be pulled out when the sun comes out.

Mourning? Not Me, Not Yet

Jerusalem, February, 1999   I just can't find it in my heart to share the mourning of many of my countrymen today. Flags fly at half mast here. Official cabinet communiques and newspaper editorials extol the departed leader. Teenagers gather tearfully in Tel Aviv's main square to light memorial candles. Israel's main Internet service provider has an icon on its site leading users to a spot where virtual candles may be lit, and babies born here yesterday were named after the deceased.

Israel watchers may be forgiven for recalling the dark days following the 1995 murder of Israeli leader Yitzhak Rabin. But today's mourning rituals are for a neighboring monarch, unelected, using the claim of direct descent from the prophet Mohammed to legitimize his rule, a man who immediately following the Six Day War, on June 8, 1967, exhorted his people to "Kill the Jews wherever you find them; with your arms, your hands, with your nails and teeth."

I've searched the Israeli papers to find mention among the eulogies of King Hussein's policies towards the Jewish state during the nineteen years (1948-1967) of Jordanian occupation of Jerusalem. How Jews were denied access to the city's holy sites; the destruction of virtually every one of the fifty-eight synagogues within the Old City, and the desecration of the ancient Mt. of Olives Jewish burial ground. No mention either of the 1950s devastation of Hebron's Jewish Quarter, leaving the 400-year-old neighborhood in ruins, with the Avraham Avinu Synagogue turned into a goat pen. There's scant reference to Hussein's tilt toward Saddam Hussein during the Gulf War and how he forbade Israeli use of Jordanian airspace to counter Saddam's SCUD attacks.

Leaders of the free world flocked to pay homage to a man who relied heavily on his police and intelligence apparatus to preempt dissent, a man who ruled through a constitution forbidding disparagement of the royal family, who approved laws, introduced just last year, further limiting freedom of the press.

Still, as Arab rulers go, King Hussein was relatively benign. The suave, Harrow-educated, peace-talking sovereign who married a couple of Western women, was someone the West could relate to. But that's the problem with the unelected — they present one face to the world, while the expression of the people they're supposed to represent is hidden from view — until a crisis erupts. The violent reaction of Jordanians on the streets of Amman to events of the past few days should give pause to those foreign dignitaries who came to honor the King and introduce themselves to his appointed and untested successor.

Many Israelis viewing Hussein's actions toward the Jewish state in recent years could be excused their emotional reaction, desperately wanting to believe in the possibility of living in a peaceful neighborhood. But exercising selective memory toward forty-seven years of Jordanian rule won't make that a reality.

I'll save my mourning for a democratically elected Arab leader who doesn't merely sign agreements with other heads of state, but leads his people to accept their neighbors in peace.

Har Habayit B'Yadeynu
(The Temple Mount is in Our Hands)

Jerusalem, December, 1999 For a brief ten days, beginning on June 7, 1967, Har Habayit — the Temple Mount, was indeed in our hands. But ever since Moshe Dayan handed the key to the Jewish people's holiest place back to the Wakf (the Moslem religious authority), Jewish access to the place has been severely restricted. Jews are only permitted to ascend to the Temple Mount for a couple of hours in the afternoon, and never on Fridays, the Moslem Sabbath. Jews who do make it onto the Mount are forbidden to pray there — recently a young Jewish woman sat down and closed her eyes in silent meditation. She was taken in for questioning and released after four hours of interrogations and warnings.

Yet despite these indignities, the people of Israel have been almost silent. Perhaps it's because of the "united Jerusalem" myth. Since 1967 Israel has maintained sovereignty over all of Jerusalem, yet we don't have control over our most precious possession, the site of the First and Second Temples.

But last night the silence was broken. For the first time in thirty-two years, a demonstration was held in Jerusalem on behalf of Har Habayit. Virtually ignored by the media, more than 5,000 people gathered on Mt. Scopus, right below the Hebrew University, overlooking the Temple Mount, to raise the alarm over the latest turn of events there.

From this viewpoint, high on a ridge overlooking the city, the myth is even more obvious. At the close of the twentieth century, the most visible landmarks in Jerusalem are the YMCA building decked out in lights for the "holiday season"; the bright blue cross perched atop the French church right next to the Center for

Conservative Judaism on Agron Street, and of course, the gold glint of the Dome of the Rock impassively occupying the Temple Mount.

But what was it that led Zu Artzeinu leader Moshe Feiglin to come out of activist retirement and organize this first protest over Har Habayit? The specter of the unceremonious dumping of two hundred truckloads of material excavated from the Temple Mount was just one violation too many for Feiglin to bear. The rubble, which government archaeologists said contained remnants of artifacts from various periods, was discarded by the Wakf as they opened up another exit for the prayer hall they've established in the southeast corner of the Mount, known as Solomon's Stables.

At the demonstration, protestors gawked as yeshiva students hauled up to the stage several large chunks of carved pillars and stone salvaged from the dump.

But despite the pain of seeing the desecration up close, the evening was filled with uplifting spirituality, not anger. In front of a banner which read "Har Habayit — the Heart of the People," Naftali Wurzberger led the crowd in song about Jerusalem and the yearning for the Temple. Between the speeches, the singing and dancing was fervent, as the voices of young and old alike wafted in song over the hills of the Holy City. Trumpets blasted

The Western Wall, Temple Mount and Mount of Olives.

through the soft, windless night in a wake-up call to Am Yisrael. Someone had forged the words "Im eshkachaych Yerushalayim" (If I forget thee Jerusalem) in string hung along the edge of the hill. The striking of a match made the letters slowly burn their timeless message against the black Jerusalem sky. For a few moments, enveloped by the yearning of the faithful, in this most meaningful place in the world, it almost felt as if we could force history to change.

Most, but not all, in the crowd were observant Jews. Russian and English could be heard everywhere, and sections in the throng held signs with the names of the cities from where they had traveled — Haifa was particularly well represented. One of the first speakers was Eitan Harel, a former paratrooper from Tel Aviv who had fought in the battle for the Golan. Donning a knitted kipa, he read passages from the Book of Yehezkel, as well as an account of the Golan fighting which told of the reaction of the paratroopers when they heard about the liberation of the Temple Mount.

A succession of prominent rabbis addressed the crowd. They included Rabbi Dov Lior, Rav Elboim, Rabbi Yitzhak Ginzburgh, Rav Ariel, Tel Aviv Chief Rabbi Gerlitsky and MK, Rabbi Benny Elon. Each rabbi was greeted by song and listened to with respect. Each scholar emphasized a different aspect of the struggle to preserve Har Habayit. Rav Elboim emphatically called for more Jews to ascend the Temple Mount in the permitted areas, with the appropriate preparation.

Rav Ariel led everyone in the recitation of the Shehechiyanu blessing — marking the first time in modern history that Am Yisrael had made its voice heard for Har Habayit. "Har HaBayit is God's throne," he declared. "It's the very heart of Israel — without it, we have no state," he added. A sign held aloft by one demonstrator reflected his message. It read: "Har Habayit, the heart of Am Yisrael. Our heart is breaking. Jews, where are you?"

Millennium Countdown

Jerusalem, December 31, 1999   It started a little before eight o'clock on the last Friday of the final year of the twentieth century — the throb of teeny-bopper pop music burst through my central Jerusalem neighborhood from the fancy apartment complex across the street.

The noise was amplified beyond belief — even if it hadn't been a Shabbat evening it would have been an intrusion. I was heading out to an Oneg Shabbat; so, playing the good citizen, I went over to ask the party hosts to spare a thought for our elderly neighbors and turn down the racket.

Crossing the street, I could see that the party-goers were no more than thirteen years old. Boys and girls, all dressed in black, most carrying at least a pint of gel on their heads, filed into the underground parking area which was pulsating with strobe lighting and decibel-splitting noise.

I asked the kid acting as gatekeeper if there was a responsible adult around, and he pointed to a grey-haired, snazzily dressed man who turned out to be "Abu Messiba" — father of the party. I greeted him with a simple "Shalom," purposely leaving out the "Shabbat," so he wouldn't take my request as a religious dig. I told him I lived across the street, and asked if he wouldn't mind turning down the volume since this was a residential area, not night club row. He shrugged and said, it's the kids, they want to celebrate. I foolishly persisted, and he dismissed me with a wave of the hand, yelling over the din, "You have Shabbat every week, tonight's the millennium!"

So, resigned to a night where I'd have to dig out my earplugs, I walked off to the Oneg Shabbat. It's just a few short blocks to Beit Elisheva, but it might as well have been a different city. Hundreds of people, dressed in their Shabbat finest, poured in to the community center. Men and boys in white shirts and white knitted kippot strolled through the warm evening together with smartly dressed women and girls.

The event was advertised only through flyers posted in the immediate neighborhood for just a few days, yet when I managed to squeeze into the hall, together with at least a thousand of my neighbors, it was standing room only. The flyers announced there would be words of Torah from the popular Rabbi Mordechai Elon, community singing, and light refreshments.

In the midst of the singing, led by a boisterous throng of youngsters, the crowd parted and in walked Natan Sharansky, who lives a few blocks away. Despite his protestations, the cabinet minister was given a place of honor next to Rabbi Elon at the head table. A few melodies later, the elderly, fur-shtreimeled head of the nearby Haredi yeshiva joined the table and drank a l'chaim. In the midst of Rabbi Elon's talk, his father, former Supreme Court justice Menahem Elon, appeared to complete the table.

The room turned instantly quiet as Rabbi Elon began to speak. Without a microphone, he was nevertheless easily heard. Rabbi Elon told how, earlier in the day, he had shown up at the Israel TV studio to record his weekly 15-minute Parshat Hashavua (Torah portion) talk, broadcast on Friday afternoons.

Arriving at the studio, he was told by an apologetic production assistant that there was a "slight problem," which the producer would explain. "Sorry, rabbi," said the producer. "Your program won't run today, we're already into millennium programming. Rabbi, we're part of the world now," he added.

"For them, 15 minutes of Torah doesn't fit in with their world," Rabbi Elon said. "This is the challenge facing Israel today," he concluded.

Walking back home, I could see dozens of the kids who'd spilled out of the party across the street — impatiently waiting in the darkness for the countdown to the next century. The kids at Beit Elisheva were beginning their countdown to another Shabbat, just a week away....

Inside Orient House

Jerusalem, January 2000   As public relations coordinator for Beit Orot, a development initiative in eastern Jerusalem, I regularly take people to see the outside of the lovely former hotel which now serves as the headquarters of the Palestine Authority (PA) in Jerusalem. I generally point out that any PA presence in Jerusalem is in contravention to the Oslo Accords, and the two PLO flags flying atop the building, three blocks from Meah Shearim, are an affront to Israel's sovereignty over Jerusalem.

We usually stand across the narrow street as I explain that PA Jerusalem Affairs Minister Faisal Husseini entertains diplomats and foreign journalists here. The place essentially functions as the PA's foreign ministry right under our noses, pushing forward the notion that Jerusalem will be the capital of a Palestinian state.

After they've taken pictures of the armed plainclothes guards standing at the ornate gate, invariably someone will ask if we can go in. I wave off the request as being too ludicrous to even merit a reply.

But recently, because a group I was supposed to lead through Jewish eastern Jerusalem later in the day had arranged a meeting at Orient House, I found myself walking in the midst of their ranks, through the guardhouse festooned with posters of Palestinian "martyrs," and past the guards who normally shoot me dirty looks as our minibus pulls up.

After a security check of our bags, carried out in cursory fashion similar to the inspections at the entrances to Israeli supermarkets, we are in. Ushered into the eastern wing of the complex, we pass a gold plaque which proclaims that we're in the International Relations and Information Center, donated in 1997 by the government of Japan and the United Nations Development Program.

The Palestinian flag flying over Orient House, Palestine Authority headquarters in Jerusalem, three blocks from Meah Shearim.

The conference room is unadorned but for some classy wood paneling and a large photo of a smiling Yasser Arafat. Our hosts are three suave assistants to Faisal Husseini. Rami Tahboub is clearly the most senior aide. In his early forties, Tahboub introduces his colleagues after letting us know he is the assistant for world affairs, while the others represent the international affairs department, one responsible for "Israeli and Jewish groups," the other for Asian/Islamic affairs.

Chain smoking, dressed in an expensive Italian suit and speaking an accented but fluent English, Tahboub proceeds to tell us about the role of Orient House. "Our major business is to keep contact with the outside world and to let them know about Israeli violations of the Oslo accords in Jerusalem," he says. "But we're also responsible for reducing the suffering of the Palestinian community in East Jerusalem," he adds.

Tahboub speaks for some forty minutes, espousing the PA party line on everything from confiscated ID cards to UN resolution 242. Where it gets interesting is when he airs his views on the future Palestinian state. I sit there in wonderment at the masterful Arab propaganda machine that in less than a decade has brought about a sea change in world opinion, making the very notion of a Palestinian state almost a given. Tahboub makes it clear that the capital of such a state will be Jerusalem, and the opening PA position on where the borders of Jerusalem would be defined is wherever the PA feels like defining them. "It's our decision — on the western side I would say at Road #1." (Road #1 runs between Meah Shearim and Sheikh Jarrah/Wadi el Joz.) "To the east, we could make the border on the Dead Sea," he theorizes. "Israelis would show their passports if they want to go to Jericho."

"Abu Dis (where Arafat has just finished construction of a building widely believed to be for use as his capital) won't be the capital of Palestine. The capital is East Jerusalem, including the Old City," Tahboub states categorically.

"After all," he continues, taking a long draw on his cigarette and pausing for emphasis, "Jerusalem has been the capital of the Palestinian people for more than 5,000 years."

A gasp from the Jewish group sitting around the table draws sly smiles from the three Arabs, but no retraction. Instead, they start to talk about the problems of "religious fanatics," hastening to add that, of course, they did not include the kippa-wearing men in the room. If only the religious fanatics would go away, Jerusalem's problems would be solved, Tahboub concludes. "We can work out some solution if we can get away from the religious orientation of the city," he says.

From now on, when I take groups to stand opposite Orient House, I'll be able to tell them why we won't be going inside.

Jerusalem Reclamation

Jerusalem, February, 2000   Less than half a mile from Meah Shearim, and 400 yards from Orient House, lies the tomb of Shimon Hatzaddik, who served as High Priest for forty years during the period of the Second Temple.

The small, cave-like site, lit by candles, lies in the East Jerusalem neighborhood now known as Sheikh Jarrah. Since the first intifada, most Jews stayed away from this once Jewish area, and until recently, the only visitors were Hasidim who came regularly to pray at the tomb of one of the last members of the Anshei Knesset Hagdola — the religious body responsible for legislating prayers and blessings and many facets of Jewish daily life.

But in the last six weeks, a transformation has taken place in Sheikh Jarrah. In the middle of October, several students from Beit Orot, the hesder yeshiva on the Mt. of Olives, were walking by and noticed a Magen David and Hebrew inscription on a building right above the tomb. Empty and covered with rubble, the building was about to be annexed by an Arab neighbor illegally renovating his house next door.

Further investigation revealed that ownership of the site, and a 24-dunam area of the neighborhood, was in the hands of the Vaad Haeida HaSepharadit — a Sephardic communal body whose members populated the area until the Arab riots of the 1920s and 30s drove them out.

Vaad members revealed that the bar mitzvah of Shas leader Rabbi Ovadiah Yosef took place at the synagogue in 1933, and that he taught here as a young rabbi.

With great excitement, Beit Orot founder, MK Rabbi Benny Elon, came with several students to look at the newly discovered synagogue. Blocking his way were Faisal Husseini (PA 'Minister' for Jerusalem Affairs) and veteran Palestinian agitator Hanan Ashrawi, who turn out regularly to protest any Jewish resettlement activity in the capital. When Rabbi Elon carefully explained that the building contained an old synagogue which had lain empty for many years, and showed them inside where the niche for the Aron Kodesh (Holy Ark) was clearly visible, the Palestinians slunk off.

Armed with the ownership papers, Beit Orot leaders demanded that police put a halt to the illegal building by the synagogue's neighbors, and reconstruction of the synagogue began almost immediately.

In a matter of weeks, tons of rubble cleared from the site revealed a small antechamber attached to the main synagogue, as well as a flight of stairs leading to Derekh Har HaZeitim, the street above, where a monument stands to the 78 doctors and nurses killed in the 1948 convoy to Hadassah Hospital.

Dedicated Beit Orot students have not left the building unguarded even for a single hour. Sleeping on mattresses on the floor, they watch over the synagogue 24 hours a day.

After days of plastering, reconstruction of the floor, windows and window sills, the shul was ready for its first minyan. Shabbat minyanim now draw residents of Ramat Eshkol and Maalot Dafna. A kollel (advanced Jewish studies program) has begun to learn daily in the synagogue.

As word of the reconstruction of the Shimon HaTzaddik synagogue has spread, groups from all over the city are returning to visit the tomb, ascend the new stairway connecting that sacred site with the "new" shul, and pay their respects at the monument to the 1948 Jewish martyrs.

One more small step in the redemption and reunification of the Holy City.

Bet Lechem

Bethlehem, March, 2000   Only five miles separate Jerusalem from Bethlehem, but the cultural and political divide between the two cities makes the gulf seem enormous.

Today, Bethlehem is under PA control, and like its neighboring city to the north, is in the throes of massive preparations for next week's visit of the pope to the region.

The pope will drop into Bethlehem by helicopter from Jerusalem, so the main Jerusalem–Bethlehem road and checkpoint remain in their usual scruffy state. Just past the checkpoint, manned by young Israeli soldiers hunkered down in their winter jackets, impromptu street vendors try to hawk athletic shoes displayed on piled up boxes on the pavement. The trademark Arab shuttle taxis — stretch Mercedes, battered and bruised from skirmishes on Middle Eastern highways — wait to fill up with their human cargo of workers returning to the surrounding villages.

But once past the fortress-like structure housing the Israeli enclave of Rachel's Tomb, it's a different story. Along the route from the helipad to the center of town everything is freshly cleaned and painted. Turning left up the hill into historic Bethlehem, PLO and Vatican flags adorn every lampost. Signs of recent renovations and clean-up are everywhere and the commercial area radiates an aura of vitality and enterprise.

In Manger Square the stage is already set up for the three hour mass, the highlight of the pope's Bethlehem visit. Boldly emblazoned on the front of the platform are two large signs in English. "The Fatah organization in Bethlehem welcomes His Holiness, Pope Paul the Second," and "The Palestinian Wounded Committee welcomes His Holiness in Jesus (sic) city of love and peace."

The square is spotless, as are the newly restored shops and houses along Paul VI Street, the Ben Yehuda Street of Bethlehem.

Inside the municipality building, graced by a plaque outside announcing that the structure was opened last December thanks to grants from UNESCO, US AID and the Vatican, there's a quiet sense of efficiency, despite the convergence of a hundred journalists who've come to find out how media coverage of the papal visit will be handled in the town.

The briefing starts fifteen minutes late but is handled with great patience and aplomb by Viola Rabeb, a thirty-year-old press officer of the PA. In flawless, colloquial English, Rabeb responds to the journalist's questions with a smile and definitive answers. On the dais sits a silent, black uniformed member of the PA police force, and the press packets are brought in by a young teenager in army fatigues.

In Jerusalem, the Israel Government Press Office wouldn't think of organizing a briefing without coffee and cake — but no such hospitality is offered by the PA, and even the women's restrooms are locked tight.

The final part of the afternoon is handled by Dr. Emil Jarjoui, the PA minister of religious affairs, who is in charge of the Pope's visit to Bethlehem. Jarjoui notes that the Pope's meeting with "President" Arafat in Bethlehem is a "very official program." Besides the mass and the pilgrimage to various churches in the area, the main event will be the visit to the refugee camp of Dehaishe, just south of the town. Anyone who traveled to Gush Etzion from Jerusalem before the by-pass tunnels were completed some four years ago will remember Dehaishe as the place where the Egged bus would always speed up and careen around the corner to avoid flying stones lobbed over the barbed wire fence.

Today, Dehaishe still houses more than 9,000 Palestinian refugees, kept there by promises that they will return to the houses they fled from in Israel before 1948. According to one prominent Israeli investigative reporter, the PA has erected a large monument outside of Dehaishe in the shape of the full map of Palestine. They've dubbed it the Palestinian Yad Vashem, to equate the plight of Palestinian Arab refugees with that of Jews murdered during World War II. A perfect photo-op for Yasser and the Pope.

Jarjoui announces that Arafat will accompany the Pope to Dehaishe where they will meet with residents as well as representatives of other camps. Asked about the sensitive issue of who will accompany the Pope to the Temple Mount, Jarjoui diplomatically states that the Pope will be taken to the door of the mosque by Israeli security, "and we'll take over from there."

At the conclusion of the briefing, the officials, together with one uniformed guard and one plainclothes cop, march outside, across the square and disappear into the basement of the heavily guarded, unmarked building on the opposite corner.

Waiting for a taxi back across the great divide to Jerusalem, there's time to take in the view. From Manger Square the construction of the new Jewish neighborhood at Har Homa is clearly visible on the next hill to the north. Ramat Rachel lies just slightly to the north-west, and Abu Dis is visible on the horizon. On the streets all around, new development is in evidence on every block.

Five minutes later, back in Jerusalem, it's as if Bethlehem doesn't exist for Israelis any more. It's just that place across the checkpoint which hardly anyone visits. The place where Rachel is buried, where Ruth married Boaz, and where King David was born.

Off Limits

Jericho, April 2000   On a recent April day heavy with a hot, dry hamsin, a tattered Palestinian flag drooped listlessly over the old orange Israeli sign pointing off the road to the Shalom Al Yisrael synagogue in Jericho. Down a short dirt road bordered by lush banana trees, our bus passes a guardpost painted in the same black, green and red Palestinian colors.

The sixth century synagogue with it's unusual mosaic floor — bearing the simple inscription "Shalom al Yisrael" (Peace over Israel) — lies locked behind a set of double metal doors, on the lower level of a squat, unremarkable stone building; upstairs, six stalwart knitted-yarmulke types, daily commuters from the villages of Har Brakhah and Kokhav Hashahar, are busy studying — maintaining the only Jewish presence in Jericho. The yeshivah, opened in 1991, once boasted 25 students. But since the 1994 Gaza–Jericho First agreement, PA rules for the students have become increasingly restrictive, and the numbers have declined.

That agreement recognized the special status of the site — which had been restored and reopened to the public by the Israeli authorities in 1987. It assigned the building joint Israeli-Palestinian control, and provided that access be unlimited. But in practice, the Palestinians oversee the site. And since 1998, no one has been allowed to stay overnight in the building, and the synagogue has been off-limits on Shabbat. The yeshivah students curtly describe relations with the PA as "cordial, just like Jews have with their landlords in the Diaspora."

While we're upstairs shmoozing with the students, our guide, Erna Kovus, is outside, negotiating in Hebrew with Muhammad Antar, the PA keeper of the keys. Antar is a handsome, youngish man dressed in T-shirt and jeans, who presides over the day shift at the dusty entrance to the site. Kovus, an intense woman in her 50s from Ofrah, who spends her days trying to organize Jewish activities in Jericho, is engaged in an ongoing conflict with the PA and the Israeli Civil Administration. She insists that Jews have the right to visit and pray in the ancient synagogue without payment. Yasser Arafat's men, designating this merely as an archaeological site, refuse to open the place without levying a 10 shekel ($2.50) fee on every visitor.

Jangling the keys in his pocket, Antar refuses to budge — even though Kovus tells him he might as well open up, since our group is ready to walk away, and he won't be earning any money anyway.

As Kovus and Antar argue back and forth, I wander down to the synagogue entrance. A lone bedraggled camel sits amid the foliage just opposite the site, casting a bored eye in the direction of a flock of sheep crossing in front of him. On the wall just to the left of the locked synagogue doors hangs a slightly incongruous bright new pay phone, inscribed in Arabic and English, courtesy of the Palestine Telecommunications Co. Ltd.

The argument lost, Kovus turns to us and explains that Antar is following orders from the PA's Jericho tourism boss Ibrahim Jaballa, with whom she had recently discussed the matter of access to the shul. Jaballa cited "technical problems" with the notion of allowing free entrance. When the yeshivah boys are alone, Kovus says, they are occasionally permitted to go down to use the synagogue, but everyone else has to pay.

I walk back toward the bus ahead of the group. A guard leans out of his booth, his army fatigues and gun clearly visible. He asks why I didn't go into the shul. When I tell him that my definition of free access to religious sites doesn't seem to coincide with his, he shrugs and offers, "So, I'll give you some postcards of the synagogue...."

The Rally That Came Too Late

Jerusalem, May 2000   No one knew that tonight's rally against Israeli withdrawals would take place against the backdrop of the Knesset vote for the most serious withdrawal of all — the handing over of three Arab settlements on the edge of Jerusalem's Mount of Olives — as well as the worst violence seen here in many months.

As more than one hundred thousand Israelis gathered in Kikar Tzion (Zion Square) to proclaim: "Enough Free Giveaways of Land," Knesset members voted 56-48 (15 members were not present for the vote, one abstained) to hand over Abu Dis, Eizariya and Suwahra to full Palestinian control.

The decision affects the security of Jewish residents of Jerusalem's eastern neighborhoods — Neve Yaakov, Pisgat Zev and E. Talpiot, as well as the future of the Temple Mount and the Mount of Olives — Jerusalem's holiest places. With the handover, nothing prevents the PA from taking advantage of its territorial contiguity to gain complete control over the eastern part of the city, from Bethlehem in the south to Ramallah in the north, both already designated as Area A, under complete PA control.

Knesset members must have been too busy with their deliberations to watch the news today. If they had, they would have seen a country at war. In Netzarim, in the Gaza Strip; Ramallah/Beit El, just north of Jerusalem and Shechem in Samaria, battles were fought between armed PA "police" and IDF troops. Arafat unleashed, coordinated and organized riots — as evidenced by the PA police who either stood by or escalated the battles from stone-throwing to firing at the IDF. Ostensibly started to mark the secular 52nd anniversary of the founding of the State of Israel, the violence is another clear indication of the intentions of our peace partners.

Because of the disturbances, buses bringing demonstrators from

Beit El couldn't get through to Jerusalem. Nevertheless, the square and all surrounding streets were packed with people eager to express their opposition to the unsuccessful Oslo process, which has brought about painful concessions from our side and violence from the Palestinians.

Huge professional banners, as well as home-made signs in English, Russian, Hebrew and French, faced the stage set up in the square. The podium filled up as the government ministers and Knesset members arrived after voting on the giveaway. Significantly, grassroots leaders of the right were absent from the dais. Leaders of Women in Green, Zu Artzeinu, Dor Hemshech and the YESHA Council could be spotted amongst the throngs down below, but none of their representatives addressed the crowd.

At the outset, the MC announced that this would be an orderly, respectful demonstration. Any disturbances would be dealt with by the marshals, he said. In fact, everything went off quite peaceably. Repeated chants of "Ehud Habayta" (Ehud go home...), interspersed with shouts for various government ministers to resign, were the most violent manifestations to be heard.

Throughout the evening, we received announcements of breaking news. The Knesset vote, accompanied by the information that the National Religious Party and Yisrael B'Aliyah would leave the coalition and reports of the escalating violence and explosion at Kever Yosef in Shechem, all evoked strong reaction in the crowd.

Veteran MK Rechavam Zeevi (known as Gandhi) received the most tumultuous welcome of all the speakers. In fiery tones he described how, in his view, the Barak administration is playing ping-pong with the fate of Israel.

Mayor Ehud Olmert, Natan Sharansky, Arik Sharon and a host of other MKs addressed the demonstrators, with MK Yuri Shtern speaking in Hebrew and Russian.

In a powerful gesture, Rabbi Melamed, the rabbi of Beit El, asked everyone to raise their right hands and recite together the famous verse: If I forget thee, O Jerusalem....

A 15-year-old girl, the sister of one of the soldiers killed at Kever Yosef in the 1996 riots following the opening of the kotel tunnel, spoke next. In simple words she told of her fears for the Jewish residents of villages in Judea and Samaria living surrounded by armed Palestinian forces, and appealed to Prime Minister Barak to reconsider the giveaways of so much territory in return for no peace.

The rally ended with the Hatikva, proudly sung by more than 100,000 voices echoing off the walls of the Jerusalem streets.

Dor Hemshech
(The Continuing Generation)

May, 2000   They don't have an office; they don't even have a budget — yet late last year, this group of young Israeli activists confronted head-on the Barak administration's efforts to dismantle scores of settlement outposts in Judea and Samaria. Planting themselves in front of the bulldozers sent to tear down the simple homes and caravans, members of Dor Hemshech (the Continuing Generation), riveted the attention of the world media and the Israeli public on a fundamental principle of religious Zionism — the bond between the people of Israel and the land of Israel.

This loose-knit group of strong-minded individuals, many the sons and daughters of well-known settlement visionaries, decided this was their time to galvanize and pick up the baton of leadership. The result has been a shake-up of the religious Zionist community in Israel.

Shimon Rikhlin, an affable graduate of Bar Ilan University and the most visible leader of Dor Hemshech, states the goal of the group succinctly: "The main objective of our movement is to create a peaceful Jewish revolution," he says.

In his view, the willingness to give away parts of Judea and Samaria is symptomatic of a lack of Zionist education and appreciation for Jewish history on the part of secular Israelis. He also blames the influence of negative aspects of western culture which have become so prevalent throughout Israeli society in recent years.

Rikhlin, an archaeologist who lives in Maale Michmash, wants to change the image of those who oppose giving away Jewish land.

"Maybe it's because I was born in Tel Aviv, I feel we have to reach out to the secular masses. How is it that, after more than twenty years of settlements, people still don't understand our message?" Rikhlin asks.

Dor Hemshech was spurred from talk into action by government demands to evict Jews from the small ideological communities in Judea and Samaria.

Their first public activity was a hastily called demonstration in front of Prime Minister Barak's residence in Jerusalem right after the YESHA council agreed to destroy some of the outposts. It was a risky move, since a small showing would have been taken as a sign of weakness — but the event, which drew more than five thousand participants, signaled the shift of power in the settlement movement from the old guard to their children — the twenty- to thirty-year-olds, born and bred in Judea, Samaria, Gaza and the Golan.

"We don't negotiate about the land of Israel. It's not negotiable," Rikhlin explained without rancor to the crowd.

In a show of Jewish unity rarely seen at political demonstrations in Israel, a group of four friends from Erez (three of the four standing bare-headed and one sporting a pony-tail) led the crowd in a song about building the Beit HaMikdash (Holy Temple).

Next, an observant young man named Hevron Shilo addressed his remarks to Prime Minister Barak: "If you continue along this path of destruction, Honorable Prime Minister, we will be forced to begin a struggle — a just struggle, responsible; tolerant, but determined. We will sit on the roads and sing, we will stand next to the tractors and we'll dance."

Sure enough, during the eviction of the Maon Farm settlers a few weeks after the rally, the hundreds of mostly young people who came to try to prevent the government action, used song and peaceful civil disobedience to make their point. Demonstrating another of the 'red lines' of Dor Hemshech, none of the protesters raised a hand against IDF soldiers or police who had been sent to disperse them. "I'm completely against the use of violence — there are many ways to be radical, but our goal is to build and be creative, not to destroy," Rikhlin declared after he was arrested in early December for attempting to establish a new outpost at Nokdim. "The real violence is the acts of those who would destroy the land of Israel."

Many Dor Hemschech activists are the scions of renowned families, such as Malachi Levinger, son of Hebron pioneers, Rabbi Moshe and Miriam Levinger. Tzippi Schlissel, daughter of Rabbi Shlomo Raanan, murdered by terrorists who broke into his home in the Tel Rumeida section of Hebron in 1998, lives and breathes religious Zionism. Tzippi is the great-granddaughter of the early Zionist leader, Rabbi Avraham Yitzhak Kook, and the niece of Rabbi Zvi Yehuda Kook. Together with her husband, Rabbi Israel Schlissel, she is raising their seven children in the tiny, one year old outpost of Charasha, on a hilltop overlooking Ramallah. The entire community consists of ten caravans, housing twenty adults and fifteen children.

Tzippi's commitment to work for Dor Hemshech arises out of her conviction that, for the first time in Israel's history, part of the land of Israel is being given away, and something has to be done to rouse and unite the public.

Schlissel points to Maimonides' Sefer HaMitzvot and his teachings of Yishuv Haaretz (the commandment to settle the land) as the bedrock of her philosophy. "It's quite clear that we're not allowed to give away the land," she states simply. When the Israeli government does not represent the best interests of Am Yisrael as defined by the Torah, it's up to the people to speak up.

Meantime, Oded Porat, the young Golan Heights activist, views their role in the context of the Patriarchs. "Avraham made the breakthrough — he was the first generation. Yitzhak strengthened what existed — that is our task, to establish roots, to strengthen what already exists; and Yaakov broke new ground — that will be the task of my children."

An Israeli Museum Becomes Politically Correct

Jerusalem, May, 2000   Once upon a time Israelis were proud to boast about their victories over invading Arab armies, eager to brag about the hardiness of Jerusalem's citizens during war-time sieges, and happy to trumpet their achievements in rebuilding and reuniting their divided capital. There was even a museum in Jerusalem dedicated to portraying and retelling that story, but today, in the run-up to the final status negotiations over Jerusalem's future, the museum is gone.

The Tourjeman Post Museum, once a showcase of photos, maps, artifacts and documents depicting the history of modern Jerusalem from 1948 to 1967 and celebrating the reunification of the once divided city, has now been converted to the Museum on the Seam, a place dedicated to "dialogue, coexistence and tolerance."

The old museum occupied a house on the edge of the Meah Shearim neighborhood facing east Jerusalem. Until the Six Day War in 1967, the place served as an Israeli military post overlooking the Mandelbaum Gate, which was for almost two decades the only border crossing between Israel and Jordan. The Tourjeman Post building, badly damaged in the 1948 War of Independence, served as a museum artifact itself — its fortifications left intact, the battle scars testament to the fierce fighting that took place there in the struggle to reunite the city.

From the rooftop, which housed an exhibition entitled "Jerusalem — A City at War, 1947-1948," to the main display on the second floor, "Jerusalem — A Divided City Reunited 1947-1967," to the first floor devoted to the history of the Jaffa Gate during the twentieth century, the Tourjeman Post Museum portrayed the city during the 19 years when it was divided — the only museum to do so.

Here school children learned of the hardships and heroism of their fathers and grandfathers. Soldiers saw how an earlier generation of Jerusalem defenders had fought bitterly over each rock, house and meter of the city. Kids from kibbutzim learned about the Palmach, about Yitzhak Rabin, and about how the 100,000 Jewish residents of Jerusalem lived under siege in 1948. Academics, UN personnel and diplomats came. Even the ultra-Orthodox of Meah Shearim didn't have to venture far outside their neighborhood to learn about modern Zionist history. Despite the absence of sophisticated museum displays and high tech trappings, the Tourjeman Post Museum successfully conveyed its message.

But earlier this year, the old Tourjeman Post Museum became the Museum on the Seam. It is now a glitzy showplace, the largest project of the German branch of the Jerusalem Foundation. While the outer shell of the building has been preserved, inside, the guts of the old museum, its displays and exhibits have been ripped out to make way for a state-of-the-art auditorium and the latest in multimedia displays and computers.

Today, visitors must call for reservations in order to be accompanied by one of eight guides. Trained in techniques of group dynamics, the guides lead each party through a series of rooms depicting conflicts throughout the world and tensions within Israeli society. There are a pressure room, a dialogue room and a media room — all decorated in bland grey sheet rock. A collage of old photos on one wall from 1948-1967 Jerusalem is all that remains of the old museum, celebrating the reunification of the holy city.

Whether the place should still be called a museum is a question. There are no objects or collections at the Museum on the Seam, only films and visual images flashed on TV screens and room-sized wall panels.

Former Jerusalem Mayor Teddy Kollek created the Tourjeman Post Museum in the early 1980s after persuading German publishing magnate Georg von Holtzbrinck to fund the project through the Jerusalem Foundation. Georg died the day the museum opened in 1983, but the von Holtzbrinck family continued to fund the museum.

The von Holtzbrincks are represented in Israel by Rafi Etgar, a celebrated graphic artist who designs book covers for the family's publishing house. After the election of Yitzhak Rabin and the signing of the Oslo Accords, Etgar convinced Georg's daughter Monika to convert the museum to something different from her father's original idea.

Etgar then approached Ruth Cheshin, head of the Jerusalem Foundation, with an offer she could not refuse. If the Jerusalem Foundation wanted to continue to receive von Holtzbrinck money for the Tourjeman Post, the museum would have to change. Etgar himself designed the Museum on the Seam and now serves as curator.

In an article entitled "The Israel Museum and the Loss of Jewish Memory," (*Azure*, Autumn 1998), Eitan Dor-Shav, a Tel Aviv advertising executive, argues that almost all Israel's museums are undergoing an identity crisis: "Throughout Israel," he writes, "museums have abandoned outright the story of the Jewish people, ever seeking other stories to tell, arranging their exhibits and their great halls always according to other considerations."

Today, it seems, it's no longer fashionable for Israelis to be proud of their military victories over invading Arab armies. The Tourjeman Post Museum, while not of the left or the right, neither secular nor religious, was, after all, a reconstructed army post. It commemorated Israeli wars, not peace, and thus failed the political correctness test, leading to its sad demise.

Letter from the Gaza Strip

Kfar Darom, June 2000   This is a walled city — not in the ancient sense, by choice, but out of necessity. The 40 families who live and work in Kfar Darom, some seven miles south of Gaza City, live behind 18-foot-high concrete walls erected by the Israeli Defense Forces to protect them from their Arab neighbors.

The walls at Kfar Darom were built a few years ago following the murder of Rabbi Shimon Biran, who was shot as he crossed the two-lane highway running between the settlement and the school across the street where he was a teacher.

Jews don't cross the street at Kfar Darom anymore. They climb a flight of stairs to use the sandbagged footbridge high above the road and descend the steps on the other side, closely watched by Israeli soldiers. Within the walls, built against the wishes of the residents, who say they didn't come to live in Gush Katif to recreate the ghettos of Europe, a thriving religious community attempts to create something resembling normal life. Children play in the preschool yard. Women shmooze outside their tidy whitewashed houses, and a factory employs scores of workers to process and package bug-free produce for distribution all over Europe.

The Barak administration's announcement that some settlements will come under Palestinian sovereignty as a result of the final status negotiations, and the residents' belief that other communities will be dismantled, have stoked tensions in recent weeks. "These are not very happy times for the State of Israel. There's a very heavy air of depression around here," says a former American, Roberta Bienenfeld who lives in the larger community of Neve Dekalim. Together with thousands of her neighbors, Ms. Bienenfeld, a marketing executive, took part in a general strike last week that brought convoys of settlers and their sympathizers to the capital for a day of protest against the proposed withdrawals.

But on a recent, blazing hot, clear day, Ms. Bienenfeld explains to a visiting group of Jerusalemites that Gush Katif is routinely ignored by both the government and settler organizations. "We're seen as just a bunch of laid-back farmers," she notes. Unlike many Jewish communities in Judea and Samaria that function as dormitory towns for the larger cities, Gush Katif is essentially self-sustaining. Few residents commute. Most are employed in agriculture or in one of the many educational institutions in the area.

According to Ms. Bienenfeld, that accounts for the recent decision of the minister of trade, Ran Cohen, to close the high-tech incubator where Ms. Bienenfeld worked. "He's trying to put people out of work so they'll leave of their own accord," she claims.

Ms. Bienenfeld meets us at the Kissufim checkpoint. She is slightly irritated that our bus arrived late, since the IDF insists that buses may not travel in the area without an army escort — one jeep in front, one in back. The escorts must be ordered for a specific time, and if the bus isn't there, we miss our chance and have to wait for the next sortie. Private cars, she tells us, are not under the same restrictions. Perhaps the army nervousness over buses has something to do with the fact that American student Alisa Flatow died when the bus she was riding in was attacked moments from here.

We're late because our driver hasn't been in the area since the PA took control of the Gaza Strip a few years ago. Until then, it was a 15-minute drive from the coastal town of Ashkelon to Kfar Darom. Now, despite the Gaza-Jericho First agreement of the Oslo Accords, which states that the road shall be open to all traffic, the IDF forbids Israeli vehicles to use the direct route straight down the coast. We spent 45 minutes making a detour on a road in Area C, still under Israeli control.

Under the watchful eye of our heavily armed military escort, we make our way through Arab farming areas toward the Gush Katif sights we've come to see.

Ms. Bienenfeld explains that all the citrus groves are Arab-owned. Fields and greenhouses on both sides of the road also belong to Arabs, who learned their modern farming techniques from the Jews, she says. The largest Arab structure we pass is the Palestinian Flour Mill Co. It's a vast, new building with silos in front and a distinctly deserted feel. Our guide explains that the Jewish residents noticed that the foundation had been dug deeply, and that it seems as if workers are never at the plant. "They're probably storing ammo down there, and they're getting ready to use it," she speculates.

Back out on the road, which cuts through a landscape of rolling sand dunes, Ms. Bienenfeld, who's lived in the area since 1981, notes in a matter of fact way that there is a lot of rock throwing in the area. "They shoot in the air all the time, too," she says of her Arab neighbors. The situation intensified during May, when Yasser Arafat gave the green light for "Days of Fury" and riots ignited simultaneously all over the country.

Jewish residents seem to have little confidence in the army's response to violence. In the past two months, three bombs have been detonated by remote control on Gush Katif roads as Israeli vehicles passed by. After a recent attack, in which one person was injured, Netzarim residents wrote to Prime Minister Barak demanding that the IDF be issued orders that they say would prevent future incidents. Arabs also frequently decide to close roads in the area, which isolates the settlements. "The army does nothing," Ms. Bienenfeld complains. "Their hands are tied because the minute they injure any rioting Arab, the human rights organizations are on top of them."

Quietly, preparations are underway for every contingency. Just as in almost every Jewish settlement in Judea, Samaria and the Golan, the Jews of Gush Katif are training to defend themselves, should the need arise. Rumors of a mass march by Arabs on the settlements are taken seriously here, and the specter of renewed violence is on everyone's mind in Gush Katif.

Underlining the tension, we notice a small Arab refugee camp overlooking the ocean just outside the entrance to Neve Dekalim, a community of 500 families. Given the rise in rhetoric on all sides and the sense of unfulfilled Arab expectations if the negotiations don't give Mr. Arafat everything he demands, it doesn't take too much imagination to visualize a possible onslaught. A separate road serves the tumble-down, decrepit area of the camp, and donkeys, goats and camels roam freely. There are no walls or fences here to keep anyone in or out.

Turning in to Neve Dekalim, we pass schools, a gas station and tidy, single-family dwellings. Ms. Bienenfeld tells us that many of the houses were transplanted from Yamit, the nearby Israeli town demolished in 1982 as part of the peace agreement with Egypt.

Lunching on crepes and espresso served in a cafe opened by a French immigrant couple who arrived in Neve Dekalim a year and a half ago, we hear that the majority of Gush Katif residents is Sephardic. The synagogues in town are Tunisian and Moroccan, with just one to accommodate Ashkenazim.

Our hosts insist that we visit the beach after lunch to relax. The road leading to the pristine white sand and glistening sea is lined with tall palm trees, the seashore deserted and littered with exotic shells. It's difficult to assimilate the fact that just minutes away from this peaceful, idyllic scene is the only place in the world where Jews still live behind walls in palpable fear of their neighbors.

Shabbat with the Sharanskys

Jerusalem, August, 2000   Looking across the Shabbat table into the eyes of 92-year-old Ida Milgrom, who is lovingly stroking the hair of her teenage granddaughter, Rachel Sharansky, I could almost feel the winds of Jewish history sweeping through the dining room.

There, at the head of the table in his house in Jerusalem's Old Katamon neighborhood, sits former Prisoner of Zion Natan Sharansky, tired from the week he's spent in a protest tent across from the prime minister's office. He's swapped his trademark army cap for a more natural looking, white knitted kipa. Ida, his beloved mother, is next to him and benefits from Natan's translation into Russian of every element of the conversation. Rachel and Chana, the two Sharansky children, chatter away in Russian and Hebrew. Rachel, 13, outgoing and intelligent but with a modest charm, closely resembles her mother, Avital. Chana, 11, is still shy and quiet and looks more like Natan.

Rachel introduces the white haired woman next to her as Doda (aunt) Nadia. She is the former baby-sitter of the girls and now a companion to Ida, who lives alone in an apartment a couple of blocks away. Nadia is an old family friend who worked with Avital's father in Moscow.

Further along at the table are two young men who live with the Sharanskys. They are the sons of Avital's late brother Mikhail Stieglitz, who died of a heart attack several years ago at age 42. The boys grew up in Denver where their mother Anita still lives; I met Anita several times during the dark years of the "ma-avak," the campaign for Natan's release. The elder Stieglitz boy has just finished a year of preparatory work in a yeshiva program at Nokdim and is waiting for his army call-up in November. The younger son is about to embark on the same pre-army preparation course. Avital affectionately calls them "my boys" and treats them as members of the family.

Ron Simon from Toronto shmoozes easily with the boys. Single and in his thirties, Ron is Natan's second cousin. Ron's grandfather and Natan's grandfather on his father Boris' side were brothers. Natan relates how his grandfather had lost contact with his brother after he moved to Canada. After Natan's arrest and the publicity surrounding his trial, Ron's father recognized the family name and re-established contact. The Simons became a central address for the Canadian campaign to free Natan.

Avital sits next to Ron. She exudes the same quiet strength today as when she was in the public eye, meeting presidents, kings and queens during the long battle to free Natan. Today her focus is her family and her work as a counselor to kids from the FSU sent to Israel on the Na'aleh program.

Rav Avi Weiss and his wife Toby bask in the joy of the Sharansky Shabbat moment. Avital spent many weeks at their home in Riverdale during the 1980s, using their house as a base for her activities. Avi helped her plan the campaign and to raise the funds necessary to travel all over the world to keep Natan's name in the headlines. As we sit down, Toby remembers the many weeks when Avital would rush in just moments before Shabbat, weary from her activities, and ready to light the Shabbat candles. Now we sit in front of the glow of the Shabbat light in Avital's home in Jerusalem.

Before we even sit down for the Shalom Aleichem hymn welcoming Shabbat into the home, Avi is chuckling over the memories that come flooding out recalling various scrapes that occurred during the campaign. We all decide that our favorite story is the one where Avital addressed a group of UJA women at a reception in the States.

Avi recounts how Avital told the women how upset she was at the Russian authorities who had just made some new demand of her husband. "Sweet, demure Avital, in her soft tones, told the women that it was 'bullshit,'" Avi says. "You could hear their plates drop...but Avital had no idea what she had said. I just wondered where she'd learned the word.." Avi adds. From the kitchen Avital laughingly retorts, "But I heard it from you, Rav Avi..."

It's well known that Natan has no singing voice, but he makes a valiant effort to chant the Shalom Aleichem and Eishet Chayil, aided by everyone at the table.

As dinner progresses, the conversation naturally turns to the Camp David agreement. Natan recounts some fascinating stories of his participation at the Wye talks, which he attended as part of the Netanyahu government. He tells us his impressions of Bill Clinton and others in the US negotiating team, but offers the same analysis and solution privately as he does in public — Barak should head home, and a national unity government should be constituted.

Just before dessert, Irwin Cotler, the Canadian human rights campaigner and member of parliament, arrives. We'd run into him earlier in the week at Natan's tent. We are all acquainted with one another from the Soviet Jewry struggle, but now Irwin is also deeply troubled by Barak's moves and is in Israel to offer support and suggestions to some of his old friends. Tallying up the possibility of a Knesset vote to bring down the government on Monday, Irwin notes that the pivotal vote could be that of Victor Brailovsky, now a Shinui MK, but better known to all of us around the table as a forceful former refusenik.

It's getting late and we begin to help clear the table. In the kitchen somehow we start talking about recent demonstrations organized by far-left organizations outside Sharansky's home. The protesters are upset that, when he was minister of the interior, Sharansky had ordered a few illegal Arab houses to be destroyed. (In Jerusalem last year, the government demolished 23 of the 10,000 illegal Arab buildings in the city). Avital tells us how she was taken aback to see several of her neighbors take part in the demonstration, including several rabbis and their wives. But her reaction is vintage Avital — she says the experience made her realize how disturbing her demonstrations must have been to the families of Soviet officials against whom she had protested.

Both Natan and Avital escort us up the street as we head home in the soft Jerusalem breeze. We part, wishing each other a Sabbath of peace.

All in a Jerusalem Day

Jerusalem, September 14, 2000   I returned home
yesterday from a two week working trip to the west coast of
America. Fighting to overcome the forceful ravages of jet lag, I set
out this morning to accomplish the usual pre-Rosh Hashana
errands. In the course of the past 24 hours, these are some of the
scenes I witnessed:

- In the melee just outside the doors of the arrival terminal at Ben
  Gurion airport, all heads turn as a tall, bearded American, who
  just couldn't restrain himself, gives forth a couple of healthy
  blasts on his oversize, curvaceous shofar (ram's horn).
- The most successful exhibit in Israeli museum history is closing
  at the end of October. Signs proclaiming "Ciao, Chihuly" in
  Hebrew are hanging all over the city, as Seattle glass artist Dale
  Chihuly bows out of town with the 14 creations that have
  graced the Tower of David Museum for more than a year.
- As I walk back from the supermarket, already packed with pre-
  YomTov shoppers, a battered grey truck slowly drives through
  the neighborhood, trolling for business. Sporting green PA
  plates, the wiry old Arab driver yells, "Alter sachen, alter
  sachen..." (Yiddish for "old things, old things.")
- For several hours in the early afternoon, I find myself without
  tap water. Did the authorities institute the threatened two-hour
  water shutoff to help deal with the water shortage, or did some
  incompetent contractor shut off a pipe by mistake? I'm too tired
  to go over to my neighbors to find out, and before long the
  water is back — albeit at something of a trickle.
- In town on my way to the bank to check on the status of my
  shekel overdraft, I find myself walking behind three handsome
  soldiers on patrol along Jaffa Road. As I pass, I hear the tall,

blond, tanned one bantering in Russian with his dark-haired fellows-in-arms. An appreciative restaurant worker yells out "Dosvedanya!" as they saunter by.

- A little further down Jaffa, at Kikar Tzion, I observe four slightly odd looking older women furtively handing out brown "Bibles" in Russian and Hebrew, along with invitations to their messianic "synagogue." I follow them into the main post office where Ethel, the ringleader, wearing an oversize Star of David on a chain around her neck, turns to the young woman behind her in line and with a gracious smile passes her a pamphlet. The startled young woman begins to read and then slips the thing into her purse. I make a great show of taking out my notebook and cellphone, all the while staring in their direction. They are visibly uncomfortable. Next time I'll whip out my government press card, wave it quickly in front of their faces and tell them I'm an inspector for the Ministry of Religious Affairs.

- It's now evening, and I'm still too jet-lagged to accomplish anything worthwhile. Plop down in front of the TV to listen to a spirited discussion about the pitiful performance by Israeli athletes at the Sidney Olympics (not a single medal in sight) — but wait, the highlight of the evening — all Israel is breathlessly awaiting the first episode of the American series, 'West Wing.' Here it's known as Habayit Halavan (The White House). Israelis don't know from east or west wings, all they want is some relief from the incessant talk of east Jerusalem and the west bank.

So to the close of just another day in the holiest city on God's green earth. (With apologies to Michael Medved...)

Face of the New Mideast War

Jerusalem, October 6, 2000   I had never lived through any kind of war — until this week in Jerusalem. But one doesn't need to have experienced one to know one. Make no mistake, the latest paroxysms of anti-Jewish violence that erupted here last week are nothing less than a war waged against the legitimacy of the Jewish state.

The educational institution on the Mount of Olives where I work was firebombed on the first day of the riots, and 50 border police took up positions on our scorched grounds to try to quell the fury of hundreds of Arab youth hell-bent on attacking the Jewish students learning Talmud inside. I couldn't get to work for the remainder of the week, since the mob had taken control of the road and bus service into the area was suspended.

The only way residents of the southern community of Netzarim could get in and out of their village was by military helicopter. Like most Jews living in the Gush Etzion block 20 minutes south of Jerusalem, Doug, my accountant, found himself stranded at home when the roads to and from his district were deemed unsafe by the army, following a shooting attack on a bus traveling from Jerusalem.

Moshe, an aquaintance from Gush Katif, wrote to say the scene at Rosh Hashanah (New Year) prayers reminded him of the 1973 Yom Kippur War. Men were told, "All the settlements are under attack. Go home, get your weapons, and come back to synagogue. Within minutes, the synagogue was awash in M-16s, Uzis, Galils and a variety of handguns," he wrote.

And just like every other war Israel has endured in her 52-year history, this one will shake the foundations of our society and our region. In one short, bloody week, the political assumptions of many Israelis have undergone a sharp turnaround.

Since the 1993 Oslo Accords, there has been a sea change in

Israeli public opinion regarding compromise with the Palestinians. A majority of the Jewish population had been willing to accept the idea that significant territorial concessions would be necessary in order to receive peace and security in return. Israeli politicians and the media were largely successful in achieving public acceptance for such a tradeoff.

But a few days ago, an editorial in the left-leaning daily newspaper Yediot Ahronot noted, "One would have to be an enthusiastic, gigantic supporter of peace these days in order to continue believing, to take hold of the altar of peace and continue fighting for it." The editorial added, "One would have to be an unprecedented optimist in order to quote the song `Believe it, the day will come...'"

In large measure, the pessimism was brought about by the realization that perhaps the intentions of our peace partners are not so peaceful after all. All it took to set off days of the worst bloodshed since 1948 was a half hour visit by a controversial Knesset member to Judaism's holiest site, which we share with the Moslem religious authority.

The perception of most Israelis is that the tinder box was just waiting to be ignited — everyone here is aware of the incendiary material fed to schoolchildren by official Palestinian textbooks. It did not come as a big surprise that teenagers were in the forefront of the violent outbursts. The New York Times reported in a front page story last August that 25,000 children aged 8-16 spent the summer in military-style training camps throughout the PA, where they were trained in the art of guerrilla warfare. Taman Sabeh, a 50-year-old woman in Nablus, told an AP reporter: "If I had 20 children, I would send them all down (to fight), I wouldn't spare any of them. We're not scared of death."

But what did surprise many of us was the participation in the war by thousands of Israeli Arabs, citizens of the state. It dawned on us that Israeli Arab citizens of Jaffa and Nazareth, who started shooting at Israeli police and troops and destroying Jewish property there, do not identify themselves as Israelis but as Palestinians. We were shocked to discover that there are Israeli voters who support the goals of Hamas and Islamic Jihad.

Dan Margalit, a prominent left-of-center journalist, wrote: "...the absence of any voices in the Israeli Arab community publicly calling for an end to the violence gives rise to the suspicion that the members of this community constitute a fifth column."

Israelis of all political beliefs were likewise stunned to discover that our defense forces, among the best-trained and -equipped in the world, could not keep the roads open to Jewish traffic, nor prevent citizens of Jewish towns and villages from being imprisoned in their homes, nor guarantee us access to our holiest places.

Yes, they did everything in their power to offer us safety. But their hands were tied, and they faced restrictions that did not allow them to actualize their full capability to protect us. The spectacle of the Arab instigators of conflict moving freely throughout the country, while the defense forces declared numerous roads closed to Jews, will certainly cause political reverberations for Prime Minister Ehud Barak.

It was not only opposition leaders who expressed outrage at Barak's trip to Paris to meet Arafat at the height of the violence. Barak is widely perceived to have failed to guarantee Israel's security and to take the necessary decisions to halt the war.

Doug, Moshe and I and hundreds of thousands of Israelis had our eyes opened to a new reality by the terrible events of the past week. It's going to be a lot more difficult to persuade many of us to accept the assurances of our leaders when it comes time to signing the next agreement.

Day of Rage

Jerusalem, October 6, 2000   Yesterday the terrorists warned that today would be a Day of Rage in Jerusalem. (As if any day in the past week has not been.) Friday is the Muslim Sabbath, so the focal point of the violence was once again the Temple Mount.

Arab leaders announced they were busing in thousands of their co-religionists for morning prayers, and the Israeli police responded with an announcement that they would stay back, in order not to impede the worship or provoke a violent reaction to their presence. Permission was given for the Palestinian "police" to take up position on the Mount, and all waited anxiously for the spectacle to unfold.

Jews have largely stayed away from the Kotel this entire week, leading the rabbi of the site, Shmuel Robinovitch, to issue a statement urging Jews to return during the Yamim Noraim (days between Rosh Hashana and Yom Kippur). "It's a terrible feeling to see the Wall so empty — certainly not what it's like every other year during the Ten Days," he said.

Today, with all the warnings, few people showed up. At around noon, when prayers at the Dome of the Rock let out, dozens of Arab youth ran directly to the top of the wall above the Kotel and started throwing rocks. Israeli police told all Jews to leave the area, leaving the Kotel area completely empty, except for the presence of Rabbi Benny Elon, member of the Knesset and founder of Yeshivat Beit Orot. Rav Benny's stand reminded me of the lone figure in Beijing's Tiananmen Square, the one man who had the courage to face down the tanks of the Chinese Army and who drew the attention of the world to the situation in his country.

Rav Benny used his immunity as an MK to refuse the police orders, and he stood praying alone at the Kotel as the rocks rained down.

The Israel Radio reporters on the scene were incredulous. "There are no Israeli police at the Mughrabi Gate," they reported. "They're just allowing these kids to continue to throw stones and bottles." "Oh, but they're not massive rocks like last week," another reporter retorted.

After a few minutes the action switched to the Lion's Gate on the eastern wall of the city — the gate through which the paratroopers liberated the Kotel in 1967. Here, the shebab (young Palestinian thugs) attacked and burned an Israeli police station, resulting in the injury of tens of police who'll end up spending Shabbat in Hadassah hospital's Mount Scopus facility.

Latest reports are that the Kotel is re-opened to Jews and dozens of yeshiva students from the Old City are in the plaza.

I am not surprised to read the Associated Press headline of this morning's events: "Israeli police fire on Palestinians after prayers."

For the past two nights the southern Jerusalem suburb of Gilo has been the scene of sporadic shootings into Jewish apartments. The residents took to the streets last night and today to protest the lack of security. IDF spokespeople responded by telling those living in the area that the shooting was coming from Beit Jala, in Area A — under full Palestinian security and civilian control. In other words, tough — we're not going in after them.

Erev Yom Kippur

The Old City, October 8, 2000   Today I made a pre-Yom Kippur visit to the Kotel. As reported earlier, the Rav of the Kotel had issued a call for Jews to come to the site. Several congregations have announced that they will be walking there en masse for ne'ilah (the closing service of Yom Kippur) tomorrow, but I'm not sure I'll have the strength for that one, so I decided to go today instead.

My normal path to the Kotel is to walk through Jaffa Gate and then down through the shuk (market), past the store of my friend Eli, the only Jewish shopkeeper on Rehov Hasharsheret (Street of the Chain); make a right down the steps and emerge into the northwestern side of the Kotel Plaza. Today I thought better of it. As I wait on Jaffa Road for the 38 bus into the Jewish quarter, a bearded, middle aged man walks down the street with a megaphone, calling out: "Don't be afraid — the Mashiach (Messiah) is already among us. Pray for the return of our soldiers...."

The bus driver has the radio turned up for the short ride into the Jewish Quarter. Chief Rabbi Yisrael Meir Lau is calmly telling listeners that he is sure the shuls will be packed this Yom Kippur, and that a psak (ruling of Jewish law) has been issued permitting radios to be left on a "quiet station." Normally, radio and TV stations go off the air here during Yom Kippur, but this ruling means that the airwaves of Reshet Bet, Network Two, will be open, but will broadcast only silence unless there's an emergency bulletin, either for military call-ups or to inform people whether it's safe to walk to the Kotel.

In the Quarter itself, things are strangely quiet for the eve of a holiday. What is unusual is to see a dozen Israeli policemen and women guarding the mosque that sits next to the Ramban synagogue. The mosque has been the scene of controversy in recent weeks, as Moslems have been renovating the structure, presumably to ready it for use. But what a contrast — the day after Palestinian police helped destroy Joseph's Tomb in Shechem, our police stand guard over a mosque in Jerusalem.

I make a quick stop at the makolet (grocery store) on the square. Five of us are in the store, four Jews and a youngish Arab woman garbed in traditional Arab dress, complete with chador (head-covering and veil). This in the middle of the Jewish quarter, not in one of the peripheral areas where Jewish and Arab stores sit next to each other. No one bothers her, she is treated courteously by the cashier, and she walks out, in no danger of attack from anyone.

On the way down to the Kotel, even the beggars who are fixtures on the stairs have decided it's not worth their while to stay around. One Russian musician tries out a few bars, looks around at the deserted steps and starts to pack up.

There is, however, a significant police and media presence at the Wall. About 100 riot police are at the Mughrabi Gate, their vehicles parked in front of the exit. Down at the Kotel there are exactly four men praying, and some 40-50 women. Camera crews and reporters roam around in a futile attempt to find people to interview.

As I leave, the #1 bus pulls up, discharges its passengers, almost all Haredim, who take their places at the Kotel.

Back home, I check in with friends around the country. Dale in Herzliya tells me that, overnight, flags materialized on apartment balconies there just like on Independence Day. Debbie in Alon Shvut, a community near Efrat in Gush Etzion, recounts how both the husband and son of one of her friends have been called up. The father is in his 50's, a commander of a local unit. The son has just started his regular army stint.

Last night at an emergency meeting of Alon Shvut residents, tasks were assigned. Medical personnel and supplies were readied and newcomers reassured. Bright and early this morning, Debbie trekked to the makolet to stock up. She was not alone — by 8 a.m., the shelves of the store were almost bare, she recounted.

Speaking about the tragic deaths of so many Palestinian kids, Debbie comments that the world can't understand how we care more about "their" kids than the Arabs themselves. Several Israeli child welfare organizations have issued statements condemning the Arab practice of putting their kids in the front lines.

It Goes On...

Jerusalem, October 10, 2000   Prime Minister Ehud Barak's deadline expired last night. He'd given the PA two days to halt the attacks against IDF soldiers and civilians "or else."

The violence continues unabated; world leaders rush to Israel to persuade Mr. Barak to give it just a little bit longer, and after an all-night cabinet session with the remnants of his cabinet, the prime minister gives in, again. "This is definitely the last chance..." he intones at a news conference. Sounds a lot like a weary, ineffective parent trying to discipline a misbehaving child.

So we all brace for yet another day of horrible news. Many in the English speaking community here are still reeling from the murder of Rabbi Hillel Lieberman of Eilon Moreh, son of an esteemed and beloved Brooklyn rabbi, well-known to many older immigrants. My friend Enid wrote to tell me Hillel Lieberman was "the son of my teacher, my principal, the Rabbi who performed our wedding and gave the eulogy at my mother's funeral." Rabbi Avi Weiss in New York remembers Rabbi Lieberman as the head counselor at his parents' summer camp who had a profound influence on his early life.

Sadly, reports of Jewish violence against Arabs come in from all over the country, too. Chief Rabbis Lau and Bakshi Doron are heard repeatedly on the air denouncing violence and urging Jews not to fall into the ways of our enemies, but it's getting harder and harder to contain the anger and frustration as the terror incidents go on.

As usual, the billboards dotted across the city provide a glimpse into the mindset of the people here. Today, I notice several stark black signs in various places in the city boldly announcing: "Kahane was Right."

Next to them are some colorful posters advertising upcoming events during Chol Hamoed (intermediate days) Sukkot. Virtually the entire country is on vacation during Pesach and Sukkot, so it's a popular time to schedule trips around the country, as well as concerts and other family entertainment.

This year, as if everything were normal, the posters invite people to celebrate the ancient Festival of the Water Drawing at the Shiloach springs in the lower part of the City of David next Wednesday. The City of David is home to 28 Jewish families who live just across the Kidron Valley from the Arab neighborhood of Silwan. (Silwan was a Jewish area founded and built by the first wave of Yemenite Jews who immigrated to Israel in the 1880s. They fled during the Arab riots of the 1930s, and Arab squatters have kept the village judenrein ever since then.) This year's event, according to the broadsheet, will be attended by Jerusalem Mayor Ehud Olmert and other dignitaries.

The next banner advertised a similar Water Drawing Festival event, this one at the Shalom al Yisrael synagogue in Jericho. The ads were obviously printed before the Jericho synagogue was destroyed by Palestinian thugs yesterday. PA military forces are blocking inspection of the site, which is in an area under total PA military and security control. I wrote about this shul a few months ago for the Jerusalem Report. At that time I was upset that a PA flag was flying over the entrance sign, and that PA forces there wanted to charge us NIS 10 to go into the shul — in my worst dreams I could not have imagined the fate of this site just a few short months later.

Singer Mordechai Ben David is booked for a Chol Hamoed concert in Hebron — I've been there in previous years when 20,000 people descended on the city. I doubt they'll get that kind of crowd this year.

I felt nervous riding the bus into town today, given the overt threats by Hamas. Others were jumpy too — police inspectors hopped on the bus to check for suspicious objects. They needn't have bothered, since every rider is eagle-eyed about such things these days.

Sukkot decorations and arba minim (lulav and etrog) for the coming Sukkot holiday are being sold everywhere, with an entire street of the Machane Yehuda market devoted to just these necessary items. The haggling is quite something to behold.

I saw all this on my way to the discount Super Deal supermarket to stockpile some non-perishable food. The last time I did this was just last year, in anticipation of the now all but forgotten Y2K scare. Somehow today's preparations seem a little more real.

Most supermarkets here use Arab labor for deliveries and shelf stocking, but the cashiers are almost always women from the former Soviet Union. Today it seemed that the checkout workers and managers of the store were going out of their way to be courteous to the Arab delivery boys.

Later in the day I found out that Ted Koppel was taping his Nightline program at the East Jerusalem YMCA this evening, so I used my press card to get in to the event. In the hall, I was taken aback to see that at least 80 per cent of the audience were young Arabs. These were not just any young Arabs. Since the program was conducted in English wthout translation, these people were the American-educated, handsome, fashionably dressed, attractive young upper class. None of them was over 35. It was clear that they viewed this as their moment on the world stage and they reveled in it.

On the Israeli side, there were a few men wearing knitted kippot whom I recognized as members of the leftish-leaning Yedidyah congregation in Baka. Several Israelis represented the Abraham Fund for coexistence, and one or two student types were there too, but altogether we numbered maybe 20 out of a crowd of more than 150 people.

A large number of the foreign press showed up for the spectacle, and most of them hobnobbed with the Arabs, who were polite, gracious and civilized (unlike the reaction journalists often get from Israelis).

I noticed Deborah Sontag from the New York Times a couple of rows in front of me. Sontag's friendly relationship with several of the young Arabs was quite evident — you could see it from the body language and the interaction. They had clearly cultivated friendship with the New York Times bureau chief and other influential journalists, something Israelis have neglected.

What is also apparent in these young Arab people is a passion for their cause, a commitment to do whatever necessary to promote their point of view. These well-educated, attractive youngsters were taking the time to work with journalists, attend programs with an international audience, make their voices heard. Where are their Israeli counterparts? Why are the activists for the Israeli point of view largely from the baby boom generation?

The program started almost two hours late because of a major oversight on the part of the ABC producers. The YMCA has a policy that no guns are to be brought into their building. Since Jerusalem Mayor Ehud Olmert and Deputy Defense Minister Ephraim Sneh were part of the panel, the Israelis insisted that they be accompanied by armed Israeli security personnel. Neither side would budge from its position, so Olmert went home to pack for his midnight flight to the States, and the rest of us sat around waiting for something to happen.

Koppel and his crew grew visibly more and more anxious and finally they arrived at a compromise. We would all leave the building, the Israelis would perform a security check, we'd all pass once more through the metal detectors, and then the Israeli officials would take part in the program with unarmed security accompaniment. This caused a bit of an uproar amongst the Arabs, who started yelling about how this was an example of how they're victimized. Koppel quieted things down and we all trooped out.

When we were checked back in and the cameras were about to roll, in bounded the round, bald Palestinian bishop who directs the Y. "Wait, wait," he called out to Koppel on the stage. "There are still people with guns in here, this can't go on." An exasperated Koppel finally calmed him down and the program started. On the Israeli panel were Olmert, Sneh, and far left Meretz MK Naomi Chazan. (She was obviously there to provide a female balance to the ubiquitous Hanan Ashrawi). On the Arab side sat MK Azmi Bishara, negotiator Saeb Erekat and Ms. A.

Anyone who watched the program on ABC could see what a complete balagan (mess) it was. The Israelis couldn't help being sucked in by the incitement and grandstanding of the Arabs, and while Olmert got in a few good points, the effect was lost by the constant interruption of other speakers.

Amazingly enough, I managed to ask one of only three questions which were taken from the audience. Frankly, the whole endeavor reminded me of the people-to-people TV exchanges I participated in during the 1980s with Phil Donahue and the notorious Soviet propagandist Vladimir Pozner. Nothing concrete was said, nobody really listened to anyone else, one side lied through its teeth and everyone went home aggravated.

Peeling Potatoes

Jerusalem, October 13, 2000   The normally raucous Friday morning, pre-Sabbath atmosphere is absent today. There's an unnatural quiet as Israelis try to assimilate the reality of events of the past few days. Are we at war, or will this crisis blow over like so many before? Will the Temple Mount erupt in violence again today, or will we have quiet as Sabbath arrives?

At the newstand in my neighborhood, people avert their eyes from the horrific images on the front pages of all the Israeli dailies. The color photo shows a gleeful Arab at the window of the Ramallah police station triumphantly holding up his blood-stained hands after the lynching of two Israeli reserve soldiers yesterday.

The image has shaken even the most pro-peace process Israeli. "Where do we go from here? How do I face my friend, Abdullah? Perhaps he isn't my friend. Perhaps I've been the most simpleminded, naive person, believing in flights of fancy such as that Jew and Arab could actually live side by side. What utter nonsense," says my friend Stuart, a manufacturer's representative for a fabric company doing business in Jordan.

Many here are deeply disturbed by media coverage of the tragic turn of events. Richard Block, a Reform rabbi here, who describes himself as "a passionate center–left backer of the peace process who would support virtually ANY agreement obtained between Israel and the Palestinians," tells me he is appalled at the virtual nonstop parade of slick Palestinian propagandists on CNN and BBC. He is especially upset at the screen captions which refer to the "killing" of Israeli soldiers as if this were the result of a conventional battle or a military attack, rather than a horrendous murder.

In the center of town the tension is palpable. In the main square a spontaneous demonstration by six pre-teens is underway. They had heard about the killings on the radio. Setting down their school bags, they take out paper and markers and start shouting out: "Wake up Israel...."

All over the main streets of the city, banner size Israeli and Jerusalem flags have gone up since yesterday. Whether due to the current situation, or in anticipation of the festival of Sukkot commencing tonight, and the large Feast of Tabernacles march next week, I'm not sure, but the effect is there. This is our Jerusalem.

But in this Jerusalem it's difficult to assimilate the reality that just a couple of miles away people are under siege in their communities. It's war and it isn't war. Some, in towns in the Galilee or near Palestinian-ruled areas, have been confined to their villages for the past two weeks. Access roads are frequently cut off, travel is dangerous, and in some places gunfire on civilian homes has become routine. But in much of the country it's hard to believe that anything is out of the ordinary — if you don't turn on the news broadcasts.

I talk to Liora Silberstein, wife of my colleague Chaim Silberstein. The Silbersteins live in Beit El, the Jewish town just across the road from Ramallah. Chaim hasn't been able to get home from Jerusalem due to the road closures, and Liora is nervously waiting with their four-year-old twins for him to arrive. I am amazed to learn that Beit El residents have no shelters — they were too expensive to build, Liora recounts. Residents have been told to stay home and keep away from the windows, particularly those facing west in the direction of the closest Arab village. Several of the Silbersteins' neighbors received army call-ups at 3 a.m. today, and Chaim is scheduled for guard duty at Beit El tonight.

"I'm sitting here peeling potatoes," Liora laughs nervously. "What else is there to do?..."

Condolence Call

Or Akiva, October 18, 2000 Anna Nozich is inconsolable. Her long hair caught in an almost girlish ponytail, the matronly mother of three grown children cannot control her quiet sobs. Issai, her husband, sits next to her on the small couch, immobilized, staring into the black hole of his grief. Their two remaining children, Misha and Marina, hover close by, each with dark circles under the eyes masking handsome faces framed by inherited high cheekbones.

The small living room in Or Akiva is filled with mourning friends and relatives, all still in shock over the loss of Vadim, one of the victims of last Thursday's lynch mob killings in Ramallah.

Shiva calls are always difficult, but what do you say to a family sitting numbed by the unspeakable violence committed against their 35 year old son and played on TV sceens all over the world? The pain in the room is palpable. It hangs heavily in the warm, still, mid-October humidity of the small town near Caesarea.

The Nozich apartment reminds me of the homes of refuseniks I visited in the former Soviet Union in the 1970s and 1980s. The furniture and chatchkes have that Russian flavor, but Or Akiva is a far cry from Irkutsk, the Siberian capital the family fled from ten years ago.

Vadim was married just one week before his death. He and Irina, a soft-featured, attractive woman, dated for four years before standing under the wedding canopy together last week. Irina pulls out pictures of their wedding — pictures which had graced the pages of all the Israeli dailies last Friday. A shy looking, handsome Vadim, wearing a white satin kipa, looks out at the camera with an open smile. Irina, in traditional white, looks radiant, far from the state in which we find her just ten days later.

I'm accompanying Rabbi Avi Weiss who has traveled from New

York to bring comfort to the families of some of the Israelis killed in last week's terror. We decide to drive first to Or Akiva and Petach Tikva, where the two Ramallah murder victims lived.

Why there and not Elon Moreh, where Avi's friend Rabbi Zvulun Lieberman from Brooklyn is mourning his son, Hillel, who was killed while walking to Joseph's Tomb in Shechem? Simply because driving to Or Akiva and Petach Tikva is still relatively safe, whereas getting to Elon Moreh has become a complicated and risky endeavor. Travelling in a car with protected windows is not sufficient. Such measures protect only against stones, not bullets. We simply don't have enough bullet-proof vehicles in the country for everyone who needs to travel to and from their communities these days. Rabbi Lieberman tells Avi that he would welcome visitors: "The door is open, but the door is empty," he says sadly.

Avi, as rabbi of one of the most vibrant open orthodox congregations in the United States, has decades of experience comforting the bereaved. But I can see that even for one accustomed to confronting

Bereavement announcements cover the entrance to the Petach Tikva apartment of Yossi Avrahami, one of the victims of the lynching in Ramallah.

mourning, the deep, profound grief of the Nozich family is difficult to face. All of us in that living room grapple with the task of erasing the horrible images of Vadim's death from our minds.

Avi's words are translated into Russian for Issai and Anna by Alex Rovni, a family friend and local city council member who is helping to coordinate the stream of condolence visits by Knesset members, rabbis and government ministers. The parents nod slowly in appreciation of Avi's empathetic expressions of caring and sympathy. Finally, as we rise to leave, Issai raises his eyes to tell us that he still has a future and Vadim will have a legacy because Irina is pregnant.

It's the future of the state which is being discussed at Sharm El Sheikh as we drive off to Petach Tikvah. Later we hear on the radio that the parties have signed the Sharm agreement, including a commitment by Arafat to end the violence immediately.

Approaching Jerusalem toward dusk, we learn that the southern Jerusalem neighborhood of Gilo is under attack again. This time Arabs are shooting into the homes on the outskirts of Gilo, and one border police officer is seriously wounded. The municipality orders the evacuation of Anafa Street, and residents are offered overnight accommodation in a local school, away from Beit Jala where the shooting is coming from.

My friend Uri Bank, who lives in Gilo, organizes an impromptu protest. Uri tells reporters that he remembers showing Israeli politicians in 1995 the short distance separating Gilo's houses from Bethlehem. "I stood with them right here, in 1995, on Anafa Street, and told them that if Arafat is allowed to enter Bethlehem, Palestinian snipers will eventually decide to shoot into our houses," recalls Bank. "And that is exactly what happened today. The Israeli government has had to bring tanks into this formerly peaceful street, as if this were Beirut or Kosovo. And the Palestinians aren't impressed by the tanks — the shooting attacks go on."

And on and on goes the pain of the Nozich family.

Communities Under Siege

Hebron & Gilo, October 19, 2000   Jay Knopf is excited at the prospect of his first visit to Hebron. The bespectacled Wall Street trader on a three day solidarity visit to Israel this week is not deterred by the headlines. He's determined to get a glimpse of the Jewish community he has supported from afar but has never seen.

Hebron isn't exactly at the top of the tourist agenda these days. With media reports of nightly shootings and road closures, Hebron, just forty minutes south of Jerusalem, has become virtually off limits to all but those who live there.

For those who are frequent visitors to Israel, individuals who own apartments here or who have close family connections in the country, a Chol Hamoed (intermediate days) Sukkot trip organized by the Hebron community was a chance to look behind the headlines. Twenty American visitors joined the armored bus ride from Jerusalem to Hebron. Most had visited the ancient city before, but for Knopf it was all new, exciting and, ultimately, inspiring.

Traveling on the tunnel road out of Jerusalem, which has been closed more frequently than it's been open recently, Knopf expresses surprise at the bus itself. It's one of the rare bullet-proof and rock-proof buses in operation, but apart from the obviously thick windows, it's indistinguishable from any other tour bus.

As we roll through the terraced Judean hills, past the Jewish communities of Gush Etzion, nothing looks amiss. Efrat, Elazar and Neve Daniel all look peaceful, masking the misgivings about the security situation of many residents in the area.

When we pass the Kfar Etzion junction, it's all Arab villages until the Kiryat Arba turn off. At the side of the road, old wrinkled Arab women in traditional dress sit next to boxes of huge, succulent wine-colored grapes, waiting for customers. The flat roofs of the

Israeli tanks on the edge of the Jerusalem neighborhood of Gilo face Beit Jala, under Palestine Authority control.

two- and three-story houses on either side of the road afford a good vantage point for stone throwers, but during our journey, all is quiet.

In Kiryat Arba, the suburb of Hebron developed in the 1970s and 80s, there's a strong IDF presence and the streets seem empty, subdued. We continue on to Hebron, stopping to pick up community spokesperson David Wilder. Hebron is under curfew, Wilder explains. In fact the streets are totally empty, the casbah silent. Only the IDF, Jewish residents of the community and TIPH international observers are out and about. The curfew is lifted for a few hours every day to enable people to buy food. According to Wilder, it's the price the Arabs must pay for their violent activity against the Jews.

We stop at Tel Rumeida, one of the half dozen Jewish neighborhoods scattered through Hebron. Here, in the home of Bracha Ben Yitzhak, we see the bullet hole in the bathroom wall, evidence of the nightly shooting attacks coming from the facing hills. The 13 Ben

Yitzhak kids go about their daily life seemingly unfazed by the violence all around them. A well-manned IDF guard post across the way affords protection, but in reality, nothing can protect families from sniper fire aimed into their bedrooms. It's a miracle that no one in Tel Rumeida has been injured or killed in the twenty-day-barrage.

Sandbags line the window sills facing the hills. When it comes down to it, it's the old methods which work.

Bracha, a lean, soft-spoken woman in her thirties sits in a wheelchair with her leg in a cast. The injury kept her in the hospital for three days after an Arab driver ran her off the road. She's made her simple caravan into an attractive home. Strings of garlic hang in the kitchen and there are plants everywhere. At the height of the shooting, Bracha and her family slept in the nearby archealogical gardens, but she laughs nervously as she describes her feeling that nowhere is safe. Not her home, not the roads, not even the unprotected ambulance which took her to the hospital in Jerusalem.

Wilder makes a point of telling us that people are doing their best to preserve some normalcy. He shows us the Sukkot (booths) which grace every Jewish home, and we take part in the dedication of a beautiful new library and computer room which will serve those living in Beit Hadassah.

But the lack of visitors and empty streets have dampened the atmosphere. The regular Sukkot concert was cancelled, although Mordechai Ben David did come to entertain Hebron residents. The sukka where we eat lunch is empty, save for our group and one or two soldiers. Inside the Cave of Machpela, we are virtually the only visitors — extraordinary for a festival day. The Gutnick Visitor's Center is deserted. Jay Knopf is moved by the opportunity to pray at the Cave and can't understand why others are staying away.

We hurry out of town in the early afternoon, in order to avoid the funeral of a Palestinian killed in the riots. On the way out, three ten-year-old boys hurl stones at the bus from an alley. They fall well short of their target, and we forge on toward Jerusalem. We make it through the tunnel road minutes before another closure is announced because of shooting.

I'm with Rabbi Avi Weiss, who, with the few hours remaining to him before he leaves the country, wants to go to Gilo, the Jerusalem neighborhood under attack from the adjacent village of Beit Jala.

We meet Uri Bank at the police barricade closing off Anafa Street. We're able to talk our way onto the other side, using my press card. This morning shots had again been fired at the homes on Anafa. By the time we arrive, a small convoy of private cars decked out in flags and signs is driving around the neighborhood. The flags carry a message which is repeated to the foreign press by Gilo representatives: "We don't have any other country."

Just about 50 yards in front of the apartment houses on Anafa sit two Israeli tanks. They sit there. They don't attack. They don't shoot. They're just there. Uri, a reserve tank commander, is furious. "They're not protecting anyone by just sitting there," he says. As we stand watching, cranes are unloading 10-foot-high concrete blocks in front of the apartments. "This way the government can say they're doing something. It's for decoration," Uri comments.

Right across the street from the concrete is a six-year-old Iranian synagogue. The gabbai (beadle) is philosophical about the new view from his windows. "Last night fifty-five people came for arvit (evening service)," he says. Tonight it's questionable if the police will let anyone through.

Gilo is now the new front line. 19-year-old border guard, Shimon Ohana of Beersheva, fights for his life after being shot in Gilo, a twenty-year-old residential area which occupies the highest point in Jerusalem. If Gilo weren't there, the front line would be in my backyard in Old Katamon.

While we were in Hebron and Gilo, the ceasefire negotiated at Sharm completely disintegrated in Shechem. Looks like the front lines are rapidly closing in.

Simchat Torah and the War in Gilo

Jerusalem, October 22, 10:15 p.m.   There hasn't been any gunfire for the past twenty minutes, but combat helicopters still drone overhead. Tonight Jerusalem's southernmost neighborhood, Gilo, came under the heaviest fire yet, and for the first time, our helicopter gunships blasted back air-to-surface missiles at the Arab snipers in Beit Jala and Bethlehem.

Maybe it's because there's no wind tonight, but this is the first time we've heard the Gilo gun battle here in Old Katamon, a seven minute drive away. The barrage of gunshots, followed closely by two massive thuds as we return fire, the whir of helicopters as they circle the area, and the wail of ambulance sirens are the unmistakable signs that war is on our doorstep.

My stomach churns in fear. I feel the tension in my shoulders and back. How vulnerable we all are. Thank God, it appears that the IDF has finally been given the green light to strike back.

10:30 p.m. More volleys. Logging in to the Breaking Israel News site on the Internet, I see that 12 attacks on 28 apartments in Gilo have taken place tonight. Tonight's activity has been five streets further inside Gilo than Anafa Street, which has been the target for the past week. So much for the concrete barriers I saw being lowered into place last Thursday afternoon. More than one hundred residents of Anafa Street have taken up the offer of accommodation from the empty hotels in town. So far, there are no Israeli casualties among Gilo residents, apart from one man who was grazed by a sniper's bullet last Friday night as he walked into his apartment.

Israel Radio's Reshet Bet reports that the IDF told residents of Beit Jala to leave their homes before the IDF would start its bombardment. (I'm almost certain this item will be left out of the BBC and CNN news).

So, back to Simchat Torah 5761. In Israel, Shemini Atzeret and

Simchat Torah are celebrated on the same day. This year that day happened to be Shabbat, too, so it was a full day's simcha. Since the start of hostilities, Shabbat and Yom Tov have proven to be essential to maintaining mental health. The absence of news bulletins, peace and quiet in the neighborhood, and a healthy dose of spiritual sustenance do wonders for the soul.

On Friday, right before Shabbat, a psychologist from Haifa University was interviewed on the radio. He warned of the onset of the "post holiday" syndrome for many Israelis. It's kind of like the post Xmas/New Years phenomenon in the rest of the world. Most people have been off work all week and on a limited schedule since before Rosh Hashanah, so the return to reality could be quite a shock.

This year, the psychologist noted, things could be worse, since most of us haven't exactly had a relaxing holiday period full of trips and entertainment. Remember, he was speaking the day after we experienced the shock of the death of 64-year-old Rabbi Binyamin Herling, left bleeding on a hill near Mt. Eval for hours after a Palestinian attack.

The psychologist gave some tips for staying on top of things. The main advice he had for these trying times was to maintain normal activity as much as possible. "It's OK to listen, to watch the news," he said. "But there's no reason to subject yourself to watching the same images ten times a day." People should be going to concerts and football matches and sitting in cafes, otherwise we're just giving them what they want, he added. I must say, I found his words comforting, since I'd spent the entire morning glued to the radio, trying to understand how yesterday's tragedy could have occurred.

Walking into shul, I feel the tension dissipate. My shul is one of a handful of orthodox synagogues in Jerusalem where women can fully participate in the simcha of Simchat Torah, so the place is absolutely jammed. To make room for the hakafot (circuits with the Torah), the chairs are cleared away. All, apart from a dozen older women, stand through the entire Kabbalat Shabbat and the Ma'ariv evening service. The singing is especially heartfelt and intense. They must have heard us sing Lecha Dodi, welcoming Shabbat five blocks away. It's such a release to experience the spiritual high of praying together with a congregation of hundreds of voices, where everyone understands exactly what he or she is saying.

As we start to take out the Torah scrolls for the hakafot, the words we sing are full of meaning: "Please, God, save now. Please God, bring success now. Please, God, answer us on the day we call." We go on to cry out: "God will give might to His people. God will bless His people with peace."

[11:10 p.m. The guns are not yet silent. I can hear them even with the windows closed against the night air. Radio and TV stations have broadcast announcements of the bombardment, with appeals for residents to stay calm.]

After two hakafot, the women take over the Beit Midrash, and the men spill out to dance in the street. Despite the threats here, nobody thinks twice about dancing with the Torah in the streets. With the increase in anti-Semitic attacks all over the world, I doubt there are many communities where they'll be taking to the streets this year.

I leave after a few hakafot to go visit a friend who is staging a lone, hastily organized protest demonstration outside the prime minister's residence in nearby Rehavia. Yehiel Leiter, an American-born activist living in the Samarian community of Eli, left his wife and seven children to spend Yom Tov on Ehud Barak's doorstep. Yehiel, a tall, handsome, articulate man, who was released from reserve duty last Tuesday, is outraged by the death of Rabbi Herling. He finds it inexplicable that the IDF left the rabbi to bleed to death for five hours, in order not to kill Palestinians who attacked Rabbi Herling's group. Yehiel believes it was a political decision made at the highest levels, in order not to incur the wrath of world public opinion, and he's determined to make some kind of protest. As we lean on the railings and shmooze, several sympathizers walk over with food and drink, and Yehiel feels encouraged. He hands out copies of columnist George Will's most recent article, translated into Hebrew.

I stop by again on Shabbat morning while going to the Kotel. It's drizzling and cool, but Yehiel is upbeat and grateful for the words of support from dozens of people walking by on their way to shul.

All is quiet in the Old City. The largest group of people around consists of Romanian workers enjoying their day off, splayed along the low wall in front of David's Tower, chugging cans of Carlsberg beer.

During lunch with former Seattleites in their apartment in the Jewish Quarter, the atmosphere is warm and light hearted. We eat, sing and shmooze and purposely try to avoid too much conversation about "the situation." One of the yeshiva students from Seattle brings over a friend who's on medical leave from the army. Nate is just 19, but his premature baldness makes him look a lot older. He's from Chicago and signed up for 14 months of service to the country. Of late, Nate has been seeing action in Jericho, but he prefers to talk about the wild Simchat Torah behavior of some of the rabbis at the yeshiva where he was studying until his army service began.

None of the students at the table express any desire to go back to the States because of the unrest, but they all know others whose parents have summoned their offspring home. Unfortunately, many tourists have chosen to stay away too, forcing some hotels to close down completely and others to lay off workers. Every taxi driver complains about the lack of business — but some have managed to second themselves to the foreign press crews roaming the country, and they can be seen driving around with the hoods of their vehicles emblazoned with the word "TV" written in duct tape.

One organization which didn't cancel its Sukkot activities was the International Christian Embassy's Feast of Tabernacles group. I went to their closing event at Binyanei Haooma on Saturday night. What a spectacle! It was SRO, as the slightly hokey pageantry unfolded. By the end of the evening five thousand people were on their feet singing Hine Ma Tov and Oseh Shalom Bimromav with gusto. Unfortunately, the overt missionary material from an assortment of well-funded associations at the booths in the hall downstairs soured the evening.

[It's past midnight and the sounds of battle seem to have stopped for the night. Once again, a minor miracle — no Israeli casualties reported.]

Notes from the Front

Jerusalem, October 24, 2000

- Driving along to the press center in the early afternoon, I look in the rear view mirror and see an aquaintance from Seattle in the car behind me. Martin, a technical writer in his late twenties, who made aliya four years ago, is dressed in his army fatigues. He's just one of the thousands of reservists who've been pulled from their day jobs for a stint back with their army unit.

- The war has crossed over into cyberspace. Now the "e-ntifada" has been launched. Last night, Israel's major Internet service provider was sabotaged and almost knocked out of service. Only the intervention of a couple of astute Netvision techies prevented the crash of the system. Not to be outdone, Israeli hackers have done a job on several Arab sites. The Hizbullah site, for example, now features a statement on its home page lauding Jewish claims to the land of Israel.

- The Jerusalem press center is now based at the Isrotel on Jerusalem's Jaffa Road. Daily briefings are held there by Israeli officials who try to combat the slick, well-financed and well-crafted Arab PR onslaught. After more than three weeks of generally negative press toward Israel, the powers that be seem to have finally caught on to the importance of a pro-active Israeli PR campaign.

  This afternoon, three native English-speaking IDF spokesmen in uniform could be seen chatting with reporters in the lobby of the Isrotel. The news board is covered with English announcements offering journalists video footage of PA atrocities of one sort or another, and advertisements for bullet-proof vests and flak jackets. There's even a refreshment table, complete with espresso machine and an assortment of cookies and cake.

- On my way home from the press center I stop at a coffee bar in town. Over a latte I open the mail I picked up on my way out this morning. My absentee ballot for the US elections is there, along with a voter's guide. Idly flipping through the guide I can't help laughing out loud at some of the initiatives for which I'm being asked to vote. They all seem so trivial in light of the issues confronting us here in Israel.

- Back at the battle scene, Arutz 7 radio reports that Jerusalem resident Ronen Ben-David told its news service:

> We have an Arab maid from Bethlehem, and I called her a couple of days ago to find out how she was doing. She told me that she's having trouble getting food, and that one of her main problems is that she has to hide her children from people who keep coming around looking for children to take to the riots. She said that the men promise the parents that if anything happens to their children, food will be brought to the families. She told me this without any ulterior motives, and I have no doubt that she was telling the truth. I didn't want to ask any further details, so as not to arouse suspicion, and I fear for her safety as well..

- We are rapidly approaching the fifth anniversary of the murder of Yitzhak Rabin zt"l. Funds have been allocated to schools for memorial candles. One full page ad taken out by a private citizen in a Jerusalem Hebrew weekly announces: "Leftists!! On the 4th of November when you light your memorial candles, Don't Forget: Who Caused the arch murderer Arafat to be so close to the threshold of our houses; Who gave us 40,000 armed murderers; etc., etc." At the bottom of the page, the author, Asher Turgeman, addresses "Beilin, Sarid, Peres — You Wanted Peace Now..You Bought us Lebanon Now." Turgeman closes with the line: "And a Special Thank You to Shimon Peres for a New Middle East!"

- Many Jerusalemites visit the besieged neighborhood of Gilo to express their solidarity with the embattled residents there. Everyone remarks on the miraculous fact that only one border policeman, Shimon Ohana, 19, has been seriously injured in the nightly shootings.

- At a meeting of the American and Canadians in Israel Computer Club last night, Steve's mobile phone rang. Apologizing to the group, he left the room to take the call. As he expected, it was his frightened teenage daughter calling from their home in Gilo. A few streets away the bullets and missiles had started to fly, and she wanted to know when her dad would be home.

- The list of groups cancelling trips here grows every day. The Stuttgart State Opera announced the cancellation of its production which was to have opened in Tel Aviv on Saturday night. But 2,000 Japanese employees of Nikken Inc. are here as planned. More than 1,000 hotel employees have been laid off and all the major hotels in Nazareth have closed.

- Winter has arrived in most of the country. Below normal temperatures and a decent amount of rain have not quelled the violence, but they have restored the faith of those who prayed for rain on the Shemini Atzeret/Simchat Torah holiday last Shabbat.

Just another day at the front....

More Normal, Less Normal

Jerusalem, October 26, 2000   The number of Israelis who have not been affected in some way by four weeks of violence, destruction and disruption is growing smaller by the day.

For those living in areas where nightly shooting and daily stone throwing have become almost routine, the situation is taking its toll. Anita in Tekoa told me today she's resigned to the idea that the direct road between Tekoa and Jerusalem will remain closed for the duration of the hostilities. The road hasn't been open in four weeks. It means that a routine trip to the city which used to take 30 to 40 minutes now takes at least one and a half hours — and that's only if you're familiar with the back roads. Her son, who attends school in Jerusalem, no longer has the freedom to hang out with his friends after school. There's one bus with protected windows provided by the regional council which picks up the school kids from Tekoa and neighboring communities.

Social workers and pyschologists have been sent to Psagot and Gilo where the nightly barrages of gunfire have unnerved some residents. Some are considering the offer of kibbutzim in the northern Galilee which have invited Giloans to use their guest house facilities for free.

For others, the hardship is economic. The domino effect of the sudden halt in tourism can be seen all over. Hotels close, workers are laid off. Restaurants and shops in the major cities are significantly emptier than usual. Tour guides and bus companies sit idle. Then there's the economic impact of the border closures. Natan, a US born commercial plumber from Nes Tziona says that several of the projects his company had been working on have now ground to a halt because they had relied on Palestinian laborers.

Many men are still being called for reserve duty. Eli, the forty-something moderator of a newslist for immigrants posted the following comment upon his return to civilian life after two weeks of duty:

> As far as the past two weeks I can only tell you that for some reason much of the violence (Arab sniper fire, attacks on vehicles, etc.) is not even reported by Israeli news. Maybe it is a good thing.
>
> Considering the tensions many of us are going through I would probably recommend that someone start a temporary discussion group for all these type of topics and to deal with the difficulties of dealing with our children (what to tell them) and the feelings that no matter what we do we will be blamed for it.

Even those Israelis who've given up on politics in favor of sport cannot remain unaffected. The European Basketball League cancelled a game tonight which was to have pitted Hapoel Yerushalayim against Real Madrid at the Teddy Stadium just down the hill from Gilo.

Then there are the Shas party activists who suspended a hunger strike which was going on outside the President's residence in Jerusalem for a few days because it didn't seem appropriate in the current circumstances. Strikers were calling for amnesty for their imprisoned leader, Aryeh Deri.

Many Bar Mitzvahs and weddings have been scaled down or rescheduled for day time hours because no one wants to travel at night outside of the big cities.

As if all that disruption weren't enough, yesterday Tel Aviv and Bat Yam experienced their annual flooding episode. Every winter, when the first deluge descends, the inadequate and illegally constructed sewer system of several south Tel Aviv neighborhoods gives way under the strain. But yesterday's flooding was even more impressive than usual. From the air, Bat Yam and south Tel Aviv looked like Bangladesh in a bad monsoon season. Hundreds were evacuated by IDF rubber dinghies, and a four year old boy drowned when his mother could no longer hold him above the flood waters. The main Ayalon north-south highway was completely impassable.

Despite the downpour, meterologists caution that we're still facing serious water shortage problems.

I learned of the catastrophe on the morning news. But I almost dropped my coffee cup when I tuned in half a minute after the start of the broadcast. All I heard when I turned on the radio was hysterical screaming about, "I have nothing left. No home, nothing." The announcer came on intoning that 300 people have been evacuated in Tel Aviv. Of course my immediate thought was that the Arabs had started shooting in Israel's largest central city and that everything had escalated to a new level. Despite the misery of the flooded out families, I was almost relieved to learn from the announcer's next sentence that we were talking about flooding, not bombing.

But in spite of all the tension, many organizations are making an effort to conduct their normal activities. A few nights ago I went to a meeting of the AACI computer club, where a congenial group of middle aged computer nerd wannabes did their best to impress each other by quoting the megs, pixels and size of their latest hardware purchases.

Tonight I went to the opening of the magnificent new Mercaz Shimshon, a cultural arts facility designed by renowned architect Moshe Safdie, which adjoins Beit Shmuel, the center for the World Union for Progressive Judaism. The Reform complex is on prime property next to Jerusalem's Hilton Hotel in the Mamilla area, overlooking the walls of the Old City. The building isn't quite ready yet because Palestinian construction workers have not been coming in to work lately, but movement leaders decided to go ahead with the event.

The opening event was a free concert by the Israel Camerata, followed by a fabulous reception in the covered elegant courtyard. Many of the foreign invited guests failed to show, but the rest of us who were drawn to the free event by the prospect of a serene evening of classical music and good food were not disappointed.

So, life goes on — but for the time being it's more normal for some, less normal for others under direct fire.

The Media War: Who is the Enemy?

Jerusalem, October 31   Raanan Gissin should be as much of a household name by now as Hanan Ashrawi, the ubiquitous Palestinian spokeswoman.

Gissin, a reserve colonel IDF spokesperson with impeccable American English, is one of Israel's best weapons in the war for public opinion. Handsome in a craggy, military way, Gissin expounds Israel's case in measured but forceful sound bytes.

But after four weeks of a grinding media battle, Gissin's appearances are sporadic at best. A few spots on CNN, most notably delivering a blow-by-blow account of IDF helicopter gunner action over Ramallah the day of the notorious lynching. One or two brief appearances on the US networks. But whose fault is it that effective spokesmen like Gissin are not fully utilized?

Is it, as many Jews seem to believe, the natural anti-Israel tendencies of most members of the Fourth Estate, or may the blame be placed on Israel's failure to acknowledge the need for hasbara (propaganda)? Have domestic politics played a role in determining who speaks out on Israel's behalf?

The consensus among English-speaking immigrants here, those on the left and on the right, is that Israel's "hasbara" is a dismal failure. Anglo-Israelis hear from friends and family back in the States, England and South Africa about the lack of media balance and sometimes willful distortion of events presented with no Israeli response.

The Israeli government has lodged official complaints against CNN and the BBC for unbalanced coverage, but is anyone planning a proactive media strategy, rather than reacting to the barbs thrown our way?

In an interview yesterday at Jerusalem's Isrotel, the nerve center of Israel's efforts to engage the foreign press in positive interaction,

Gissin told me in no uncertain terms how he perceives things. Dressed in civvies, with a California State Assembly pin adorning the lapel of his dark green jacket, Gissin is a lot less formidable than he appears on TV in his neatly pressed army uniform.

It's the opening day of the winter Knesset session, and Gissin is squeezing in an interview before he heads back to the side of his civilian boss, Arik Sharon. "I'm a strategic advisor to Sharon," Gissin acknowledges.

His manner is animated and slightly aggressive as he launches into an explanation of the causes of Israel's rotten press coverage. He cites the hackneyed phrase that Israel is no longer the underdog, and goes on to concede the superior planning and media strategy of the Palestinians. "They've concentrated all their resources on the effort to win public opinion," Gissin claims. The daily violence is played out for the cameras, which explains why the kids with stones come out early in the day, the Tanzim with rocks and fire bombs later, finally the snipers strike at night. "Shooting doesn't look good on TV," Gissin notes with a slight smile.

Becoming more animated, the colonel explains how dissatisfied he is with our PR infrastructure. He's definitely not alone. Veteran commentator Yosef Goell, in an article entitled 'Our Irrelevant Foreign Ministry,' writes: "We seem to have learned nothing from a quarter century of hasbara failures."

It was two weeks into the violence before Nachman Shai, director of the Science, Culture and Sports Ministry, was drafted to head up and coordinate the activities of the Foreign Ministry, Government Press Office, IDF, police and the Prime Minister's Office. "But they didn't give him any authority," Gissin complains. "He has no power to impose policy."

Gissin would have preferred a "Czar," a personality, someone like Benjamin Netanyahu. "Give him the resources and he'd get on with it," he says. But neither Gissin nor Netanyahu can claim the trust of the Barak administration. So that's why you're more likely to see cabinet ministers Yossi Beilin or Shimon Peres, authors of the ill-fated Oslo Accords, on international TV in the slightly ludicrous role of defending Israel's battle against their old buddy and peace partner, Yasser Arafat.

But Gissin doesn't have to wait for Shai's office to set him up with interviews. He has plenty of contacts from his twenty years in the IDF spokesman's office dealing with the foreign press. Still, Gissin has nothing good to say about the way the media treat him. "I never have the last word," he says. "They'll give Ashrawi and (Saeb) Erekat five minutes of uninterrupted time, and I'll get a thirty second sound byte." Gissin singles out Sky News and the BBC as the worst for Israel. "CNN is a mixed picture, and the US networks are willing to give us more time," he adds.

As we wrap up our conversation, uniformed young men start to set up for the daily afternoon briefing. Most are native English speakers who have been called up for reserve duty to help out in the crisis. They man the temporary IDF spokesman's office in the press center, answering questions and try to persuade journalists to accompany IDF jeeps on patrol in the hot spots. So far only one, Jack Kelley of USA Today, has taken them up on the offer.

The PA hasbara machine is obviously more effective. Reporters from the Washington Post and New York Times have both filed stories from behind the lines of the PA rock throwers.

Gissin is involved in training the new generation of Israel's media spokesmen and women. "The messages have to be basic," he emphasizes. "They want to win this war, we only want to survive it."

Now We're Really at the Front

Jerusalem, November 1, 2000   Three Israeli soldiers were killed today — two in a fierce battle at El Khader a village overlooking Efrat, the third near Jericho.

Meanwhile, another family of American immigrants mourns a son. This time it is the sad turn of the Gilmore family in Moshav Mevo Modiin, best known as the Carlebach moshav. Esh Kodesh Gilmore, 25, father of an 18-month-old girl, was shot at point blank range in the National Insurance Office in East Jerusalem two days ago. A computer programming student, Esh Kodesh was working as a security guard to support his wife, Inbal, and baby.

The Gilmores made aliya from New Jersey in 1970 and married in 1974. Esh Kodesh was the eldest of their six children.

Esh Kodesh's father, Reuven, said he felt disgusted by the government reaction to the murder of his son. "They bomb an empty building in exchange for my son's life?" he asks in his grief.

The National Insurance Institute where Esh Kodesh was killed is responsible for serving 220,000 Arabs living within the Jerusalem municipality. 19,376 families receive child allowances from the Israeli institution, 1,439 disability allowances are paid, and 7,573 Arab senior citizens receive Israeli pensions.

Meanwhile, the Jericho casino has finally fallen victim to the war. For the past few weeks the roof of the building was used as a sniper post. Yesterday the management decided to close indefinitely. Today, the hotel next door was used as a base for Arab snipers to fire on the nearby Jewish community of Vered Jericho.

As fighting in Gilo intensified, an elementary school in the neighborhood came under fire from Beit Jala. A member of the parents' committee interviewed on Channel 1 declared: "We've requested special defense but we've received nothing. Barak isn't doing a thing... He doesn't even know what to do. Our kids are under attack in broad daylight!" In the meantime, when Jerusalem Mayor Ehud Olmert came to visit, he was forced to hit the ground, together with a Jerusalem Post reporter, as the firefight ignited.

CNN reporter Ben Wademan was shot in the waist yesterday while on the Palestinian side of the Karni crossing near Gaza. Israeli authorities immediately offered to evacuate him to an Israeli hospital, but Wademan chose to be treated at a hospital in Gaza City. Today, he was quietly transferred to Hadassah Ein Kerem, where he's listed in moderate condition. The bullet exited his body underneath his arm, so there's no way to confirm just who took a potshot at the reporter.

On Dubnov Street near the Jerusalem Theater, a couple of blocks away from my apartment, a bomb placed underneath a car exploded tonight. One person was treated for shock.

Incredibly, while the violence rages on, Shimon Peres flies down to Gaza to meet Arafat. According to one reliable source, an Arafat aide threatened that if Peres would not arrive, the PA would consider it a declaration of war.

Peres explained to a security cabinet meeting earlier today that if the Palestinian economy were improved via business investments, then things would calm down. He said that when there is shooting, Israel should talk.

Rabbi Yehiel Eckstein arrives with a small multi-faith delegation from Chicago to announce the immediate delivery of a $3 million check for Israeli welfare projects raised from US Christians. Eckstein promises that an additional $12 million will be raised over the next few months.

A company commander serving near Ramallah recalls how a Jewish contractor working on army fortifications during a recent riot looked through his binoculars and saw his own Palestinian laborers throwing rocks and firebombs at them.

"That one does my plastering, and that one's my driver," the commander recalls the contractor saying.

More than Just a Bar Mitzvah

Jerusalem, November 2, 2000 It was a day that no one in the Goldenberg family will ever forget.

It started out as the bar mitzvah celebration of their only son, Evan, but it turned out to be a day marked by the emotional highs and lows of life in Jerusalem in violent times.

In the morning, Mark and Deborah Goldenberg, of Beverly Hills, and their family and friends basked in the joy of their simcha — dancing, singing and bursting with pride at the entry of their son into Jewish manhood. By the afternoon they were grieving together with all Israelis over the Machane Yehudah terror attack which claimed two young lives.

What began as a fairly routine affair experienced by many U.S. teens became a far more nuanced event which was part solidarity mission, part affirmation of post-Holocaust Jewish continuity, and part sharing in both the joys and tragedies of life in the Jewish state.

The Goldenbergs were determined to hold their simcha in Jerusalem as planned, despite the violence of the past month. As the date neared, several of their friends decided not to make the trip; but their rabbi, Elazar Muskin, some twenty families from the Los Angeles area, former LA residents living in Israel, and a large group of high school graduates studying here for the year made up the more than 150 people who gathered in the early morning sunshine to take part in Evan's bar mitzvah overlooking the Western Wall.

Mark and Debbie had long cherished the dream of celebrating the bar mitzvah of their son in Jerusalem. Coming from a strongly Zionist family of Holocaust survivors, Mark recalls celebrating his own bar mitzvah just two months after the Six Day War in 1967. "I remember expressing the hope that I would come to Israel," he says. In fact, Mark spent two years studying at the Netiv Meir

Yeshiva before college and has been coming back regularly ever since.

The Goldenbergs wanted to inculcate the same love of Israel into their children. Their oldest daughter, Stephanie, is spending the year at a Zionist girls' seminary, and their two younger daughters, Alyson and Melissa, have already visited the country many times. "All my kids feel at home here," Mark says proudly.

"It's because we feel so much a part of Am Yisrael (People of Israel) that we can't just be here when things are great," Mark declares. "We have to stand together when things get tough. It's now that Israel needs our support...that's why we were determined to be here now," he adds.

Many of those who'd traveled from Los Angeles expressed similar sentiments. Dr. Larry Platt, one of Mark Goldenberg's closest friends since their childhood in Detroit, and a prominent Los Angeles Jewish community leader, said he would tell fellow Angelenos that more groups should be coming to Israel to show support. "We need to be strong, to show people we care. Our presence is more important than ever," Platt remarked, noting that between his professional and personal interests in the country, he has visited Israel several times during the past year.

Platt's daughter is also attending a Jewish studies program here this year, but there are no plans to bring her back to L.A. Felice Greenbaum, another L.A. parent of a student spending the year here, said she decided to come to the bar mitzvah because she wanted to send the message that "If it's safe enough for our kids, then we're here too."

The Goldenbergs thought about marking Evan's bar mitzvah day with something permanent, "something which would outlive all of us, just like the State of Israel," as Mark put it. They chose to commission the writing of a Torah scroll and to save the inscribing of the final letters for the day of the bar mitzvah. The Torah, dedicated to Evan's grandparents, will find its permanent home at the Young Israel of Century City. Joyous singing, hugs, and faces shining with tears accompanied the ceremony right before the bar mitzvah, as scribe Shmuel Rosenfeld put the finishing touches to his year-long project.

Evan, the blond, blue eyed bar mitzvah boy, draped in a prayer shawl adorned with silver, read his portion from the new Torah scroll with confidence. Several of the men were clearly distracted by the stunning view from the rooftop outdoor synagogue overlooking the Temple Mount and the Western Wall.

When the time came to carry the Torah down from the celebration on the first leg of its long journey to its new home, these Los Angeles doctors, dentists and lawyers made their own impromptu solidarity mission with old Sephardic men, lively yeshiva students and secular tourists. Watched by their delighted wives who clapped and sang along, the Los Angelenos drew the others into their circle as they danced joyously with their Torah underneath a tallit canopy in front of the Wall.

As Evan was hoisted onto the shoulders of a dark, bearded new friend, it was clear that those who had come from LA to witness his Jewish coming of age here at the heart of the Jewish nation were swept up in the moment. With joy and pride in his eyes, Mark Goldenberg announced to nobody in particular: "If we'd have cancelled this, I would have regretted it for the rest of my life."

Mission Accomplished?

Jerusalem, November 3, 2000   Another Unity Mission headed home last week after a whirlwind two days of solidarity with embattled Israelis. On the worst day of violence since the start of this war, two hundred American and Canadian Jews, who barely had time to get over their jet lag, returned to their respective communities to bring back a message from Israel.

Sadly it will be a message from politicians and "experts," not from the Israeli people who had little chance to mingle with the missionaires. A planned visit to Gilo today was canceled — Malcolm Hoenlein of the Conference of Presidents told guests at the closing dinner that "police had blocked the streets" into Gilo. "It's not we who were unwilling to go there..." (as reported on Israel Radio news) he said.

Not ten minutes after he spoke, three renegade mission participants returned from their own private solidarity visit to Gilo's Rehov Ha'anafa — target of Arafat's snipers — reporting that they had no problem driving a rental car to the police barricade two blocks away.

While mission organizers were careful to include a balanced array of speakers, the absence of any meaningful interaction with Israelis most affected by the current crisis was telling. Security concerns were cited as the reason the group did not venture out to Psagot, Hebron or Beit El. But English-speaking residents of these communities could have been brought in to the hotel to brief the visitors over dinner and to offer a hands-on perspective.

Several participants noted that people from abroad wouldn't come if high profile political and media personalities were not included in the itinerary. Depending on one's politics, the opportunity to be photographed next to Arik Sharon or Ehud Barak was evidently worth the 12-hour flight and sleep deprivation inherent in the mission experience.

A number of the participants were rabbis, from as far afield as Hong Kong and California. Too bad they didn't get to put their pastoral skills to use. They could have been paying condolence calls on the bereaved families of Americans killed in the past four weeks of violence, or performing the mitzvah of visiting their injured rabbinical colleague, Rabbi Haim Brovender, recuperating from his brutal treatment at the hands of the PA police. They could have even borne witness to the destruction of the synagogue of another colleague, Rabbi Shlomo Riskin, in Efrat.

Still, the rally at the kotel was a nice touch. And the group did fill the Sheraton Plaza Hotel and provide employment for the bus drivers and tour guides. (One Boca Raton couple, who had taken a trip through Jewish eastern Jerusalem last year, complained bitterly about the unabashed politicking of the guide on their bus. They moved to another bus for a visit to the Haas Promenade, only to be amazed that this guide failed to point out the PA parliament building in Abu Dis or the significance of Abu Dis itself.)

Most people in the group were seasoned mission-goers. But a few, like Oklahoman Tim Giblet, a charming and impassioned Christian defender of Israel, were genuinely excited and fired up by their initial trip to the Land. Giblet vowed to return soon for an extended visit to the place he had learned to love through the Scriptures.

Most of the participants were indeed pleased with the trip, feeling that they had made their statement of solidarity. And Israelis were genuinely happy to see them here, even if the mission of trying to grasp our horrible situation was not fully accomplished.

Digging in For the Long Haul

Jerusalem, November 6, 2000   As the ultimatums come and go, while certain government leaders run back and forth to Yasser Arafat, and the names of the various failed agreements fade out of the national conciousness (who remembers Paris, Sharm?), Israelis are reluctantly digging in for the long haul.

People living in communities under siege for more than a month have now become used to the nightly barrage from their Arab neighbors. Living with sandbagged windows has become "normal" for many Israelis in front line communities. It has become routine for travelers in and out of Gush Etzion and other risky roadways to call the Moked (regional HQ) to inquire if the roads are open. Wives in Gush Etzion and Gush Katif are used to their husbands not being able to get home after work and sleeping in the city at the home of relatives.

Almost everyone has a story of how they themselves, or friends or family, came under attack by stones or gunshots while traveling on the highways of Israel.

Yet paradoxically, for most city dwellers life goes on as normal. But the tension takes its toll on everyone, whether or not they're directly affected. Last night the Association of Americans and Canadians in Israel (AACI) held a forum with a social worker at the Gilo community center. About 45 English speakers showed up to listen to social worker Bruce Auslander explain how to access the city's social services, and how to deal with stress. Bruce told the crowd that the municipality maintains 27 offices all over the city, staffed on a 24 hour a day basis with on-call trained social workers.

It was in the Q & A session that people's real fears were aired. About half of those present were Gilo residents, who spoke matter of factly of the night time bombardments which accompany their sleeping hours. Typically, almost all those who spoke up were women, most explaining that their anxiety was not about the fear of personal injury, but rather about the prospects for any long term resolution to the state of affairs. "It's clear that our leadership has no clue what to do to stop this — we're out of control," said a youngish mother who had come from the northern suburb of Givat Zev to air her feelings. "That's more anxiety-provoking than worrying about bullets. I'm worried about what will happen to this country in the next six months," she continued as others nodded in agreement.

Another, older woman stood up to say that she had been just fifty feet from the car blast in Machane Yehudah last week. "I was able to collect myself pretty quickly from that," she recalls. "There's a different quality to that fear, but the long term thing — it's wearing me down."

Parents of young children spoke of their efforts to try to allay the fears of their kids who now attend schools behind sand-bagged windows, and who sometimes cannot go out to play in the streets and playgrounds. Auslander, the social worker, empathized, noting that it's hard to convey a sense of safety and security to children when the parent him/herself is not feeling safe and secure.

One woman from Gilo declared: "This is such a strange situation. A few nights ago I was hearing shooting from Beit Jala and cheering from the stadium at the same time!" (Jerusalem's Teddy Stadium, home to the Betar soccer team, is less than half a mile from Gilo).

For some in the group, the crisis situation has exacerbated feelings of being an outsider to Israeli society. A number of older English-speaking immigrants have a limited command of Hebrew, leaving them to rely on relatives or neighbors for information. One Gilo resident, who admitted to having been in the country "many years," said she had difficulty understanding some of the loudspeaker announcements broadcast by police vehicles in the streets. "It's like I see and hear everything through gauze," she explained.

On the bus back from the meeting I pass Machane Yehuda, scene of last week's bomb attack which claimed two young lives. The eerie emptiness of the deserted market at night is broken by the stark black and white signs plastered over the front of every stall: 'Kahane Was Right.'

Meanwhile, the Jewish Agency has started another sticker campaign — many cars display blue and white bumper signs with the slogan: 'Zionism Will Triumph.'

But one apparent casualty of the heightened emotions of Israelis today is the right of free speech. A teacher in Haifa was suspended after he initiated a petition to Prime Minister and Education Minister Ehud Barak asking to end the requirement of all educators to teach "the legacy of Yitzhak Rabin." Last week the country observed the fifth anniversary of Rabin's assassination, with memorial ceremonies and lectures all over the country. In his petition, Yisrael Shiran condemned the murder of the former prime minister but noted that "Rabin's legacy must be seen as one of surrender. We now see that Rabin is the one who was responsible for the catastrophic situation in which our state now finds itself. Our conclusion is that Rabin and his 'way of peace' are that which brought us to this intolerable situation... The man Rabin and his legacy are no longer of interest for the Israeli public, and especially not for educators and their pupils."

Shlomit Amichai, director-general of the Education Ministry, was asked by Israel Radio today how the ban on Shiran jibes with his right to freedom of speech. She said: "It is totally inconceivable that during the week in which we remember our murdered prime minister, Yitzhak Rabin, such things will be said. It is a totally correct decision not to let this man into our schools and have him discuss these issues with our students..."

Yuli Tamir, minister for immigrant absorption, asked Amichai to fire Shiran, and several Meretz MKs supported her request. Meantime, the free speech rights of Arab MKs who incite against

Israel and call for an escalation in the intifada are supported by these same Israeli officials.

Another little noticed front of the war: According to a report published last week in the Ramallah-based Arabic daily, Al-Hayat al Jadida, 2175 births were registered in the Gaza Strip alone since the current Palestinian violence began on 28 September.

The paper quoted the head of the gynecology department at the Shifa hospital in Gaza, Dr. Akram Saqqa, as saying that the birth rate in Gaza since the outbreak of the new intifada was significantly higher than in the same period last year.

We're in for the long haul....

Jewish Pride or Trauma

Jerusalem, November 9, 2000 Remember the worldwide resurgence of Jewish pride right after the Six Day War? Jews in the former Soviet Union found the courage to demand their right to emigrate; young Jews in western countries reveled in identifying with the feisty Jewish homeland; young men took to wearing kippot in public; Zionist youth movements flourished and thousands of western Jews even made aliya.

We were proud and grateful that Israel had defended itself against enemies and regained control over many holy places which had been lost to us for so long. Who could forget the pictures of that first Shavuot celebration in newly reunited Jerusalem, where thousands flocked to the Wall? Once again Jews had access to the Cave of the Patriarchs in Hebron; Joseph's Tomb in Shechem; the ancient synagogues of Jericho and Rachel's Tomb on the road to Beth Lechem. These were the images that inspired Jews the world over.

Sadly today, it's as if the mirror image of those heady days is unfolding before our eyes. And just like in 1967, the tremors will be felt around the Jewish world.

Today is the traditionally observed yahrzeit for Rachel, a matriarch of the Jewish people. But today, unlike during the past 32 years, Jews were prevented from praying at Rachel's Tomb. The action follows the destruction in the past month of Joseph's Tomb, as well as the 6th century Shalom al Yisrael synagogue in Jericho. It follows the stoning of Jews praying at the Western Wall and the subsequent temporary closure there. The pattern is clear. The PA first tries to discredit Jewish claims to the holy sites, then moves in to physically attack them, either destroying them completely, or generating enough violence to prevent Jews from coming close to the place.

Rachel's Tomb has been closed to Jewish prayers since Rosh Hashanah, this despite the fact that, according to the Oslo Accords, the territory is completely under Israeli control. Nevertheless, the constant barrage of Arab violence at the fortified ancient tomb has caused the IDF to prevent access to Jews.

Last Monday a group of 30 women and their babies took things into their own hands and walked into Kever Rachel from the Gilo Junction. Their intention was to stay until today to ensure that the site would remain open to all who wanted to mark the anniversary of Rachel's death. They were forcibly evacuated later that afternoon, with the promise that bullet-proof buses coming from the junction would be allowed in on Thursday.

Women's groups started to spread the word, only to learn last night that, in the face of Fatah threats of violence announced on Army Radio, IDF Chief of Staff Shaul Mofaz decided to cancel permission for the opening. The Tanzim terrorists openly voiced their intention to step up attacks against forces protecting the holy site, in order to drive Israel out of the area, as was the case recently in Joseph's Tomb in Nablus. Prime Minister/Defense Minister Ehud Barak and Chief of Staff Shaul Mofaz ordered the Israeli retreat from Joseph's Tomb which today remains under PA control.

The situation at Kever Rachel was the lead item on the morning news talk shows today. Rabbi Ovadya Yosef issued a halakhic ruling that women should not go to the Kever because of the potential threat to life. Chief Rabbi Yisrael Meir Lau told reporters women should come to the Wall instead, and former MK Chanan Porat asked rhetorically whether people would be told not to attend today's official memorial services marking the yahrzeit of Yitzhak Rabin because the IDF could not guarantee their safety.

Despite the disinformation and confusion surrounding the event, some 200 people did show up at the Gilo Junction in an attempt to reach the site and to voice their displeasure with the IDF decision.

Police barricades completely block the road leading from

Jerusalem to Beth Lechem, some 500 meters before the Kever. A large force of border police and IDF soldiers in flak jackets, with batons at the ready, wait for the crowd. On the other side of the blue iron barriers stand some 75 photographers, journalists and cameramen. They record the frustration of many in the crowd who yell their disapproval at the impassive troops.

The group is diverse. A handful of young Kachniks (members of the banned organization of followers of the late Rabbi Meir Kahane); large numbers of observant women of all ages, armed with nothing more than their books of Psalms; a busload of members of the activist Women in Green group; a large contingent of Anglo immigrants from Efrat and a small number of Haredi men.

When it becomes clear that no one will be allowed through, many women begin to recite psalms. Some are in tears at the disappointment of being almost within sight of Rachel's Tomb, but prevented from getting there. Others start to talk to journalists, explaining their disillusionment with the situation and airing their complaints about coverage of events of the past month.

Several futile attempts are made by the Kachniks to break through the police lines, leading to pushing and shoving which almost gets out of hand. A few older women are caught in the fray and fall to the ground. After control is restored, a couple of policemen feel so sure of themselves that they light up cigarettes as they man the barricades.

Not more then 15 minutes after we arrive, a loud explosion is heard just to the east in Beit Sahour. Smoke and dust billow into the air and the media horde rushes over in that direction to get a closer look. Only later do we discover what had happened. Israeli helicopter gunships targeted a van carrying two prominent PA intelligence officials, Hussein Abayat and Khaled Salahat. Abayat was killed and Salahat critically wounded in the lightning strike.

Some 45 minutes after the explosion, a Red Crescent ambulance screeches up to the barricade from the direction of Bethlehem. The

Border patrol officer protecting worshipers at entrance to Rachel's Tomb.

hotheads in the crowd start to yell that it shouldn't be allowed through but are quickly shouted down by others with more sense.

The cameramen can't believe their luck and tear open the door of the ambulance to peer inside. In no more than 80 seconds, the police commanding officer at the scene gives the OK for the vehicle to proceed, officers quickly open the barricade to the side of the protestors, and the driver roars off in the direction of Jerusalem. Later in the day AP reporter Nasser Shiyoukhi files a report saying that "settlers" tried to prevent the ambulance from going through.

Before this incident, a busload of politicians arrives. They disembark in front of the barricades and try to push through, but the police are having none of it. Shaul Yahalom, an MK from the National Religious Party, engages in a spirited dialogue with a blue-uniformed senior police officer. With microphones catching every word, Yahalom goes through the motions of asking to be allowed to get to Kever Rachel with the crowd. When the media people drift off, the officer lets Yahalom, MK Rehavam Ze'evi, and Rabbis Haim Druckman and Benny Elon through the barrier. But none of them takes the lead to march to the Kever. They stand around forlornly, not quite knowing what to do next. "All they're good for is to give interviews and talk into their cellphones," complains a Gilo resident standing next to me.

After further negotiations, the IDF agrees to permit the politicians entry to the Kever. Only Rav Benny Elon consents to include the small group of women who had walked through the wadi earlier in the morning and who now refuse to move from their spot some 100 yards up the road from the barriers. But the IDF found even this tiny contingent unacceptable, so finally only the MKs and two Hebron women are escorted to Kever Rachel, where they conduct a short prayer service but leave quickly after police learn of a Palestinian threat. No one else is permitted to enter.

Part of the demoralization felt by Israelis in the current crisis is attributable to lack of leadership and lack of direction. What can be more demoralizing for a people than to be denied access to places which constitute their spiritual and historic heritage? What can be more damaging to Jewish pride than witnessing the destruction and defilement of Jewish holy places by those who cannot tolerate Jews in their midst?

Of course Jews have experience in such things. In a strange quirk of the calendar, tonight is also the anniversary of Kristallnacht. Sixty-two years ago, hundreds of synagogues across Germany were burned and smashed to the ground.

Jews eventually recovered from that trauma and entered a period of Jewish pride, which sadly appears to be drawing to an abrupt close. The proud days of post-1967 seem a long way off. Whether or not we can reverse the course will depend heavily on the legacy of days like today.

Escalation

Jerusalem, November 13, 2000   Today an Israeli mother of five was shot and killed in broad daylight while driving on Route 60 just half an hour north of Jerusalem. She was not the day's only Israeli victim of Arab terror. Two soldiers, both under 20 years old, and a 36-year-old father of three from Netivot also lost their lives in terror attacks.

These murders occurred hours after Prime Minister Ehud Barak and President Bill Clinton concluded their talks in Washington. Arab terrorists murdered the Jews one day after Yasser Arafat, addressing the Islamic Conference in Qatar, called on all Palestinian factions, including Hamas, to "join forces to end the occupation. Our people are determined to continue their holy war," the former peace partner declared.

The escalation of terror did not come as any surprise to Lt. Col. Gal Luft, who told a news conference yesterday that Arafat has three options to achieve his goal of creating a Palestinian state with Jerusalem as its capital: (1) terrorism, (2) a popular uprising, or (3) guerrilla warfare.

Luft explained that the PA chairman is reluctant to over-use option 1 since it would bring the wrath of the international community down on his head. Option 2 has not been overly successful to date, according to Luft. Arafat has largely failed to involve broad sectors of the Palestinian population (in eastern Jerusalem, for example). "It's always the same few thousand people who're out on the streets," Luft says.

Thus option 3, guerrilla warfare, is Arafat's best strategy. Over the long term it will produce enough Israeli casualties for the Israeli public to start an outcry, and another 'Four Mothers' movement, demanding a withdrawal from the territories, will start up. In fact, had Luft been speaking today, he could have referred to the front page ad placed by Peace Now in English and Hebrew papers this morning, calling on Barak to "dismantle those settlements that are in the midst of heavily populated Palestinian areas." The bright red quarter page ad started out by stating: "It is clear that the settlements and by-pass roads are the main obstacles to the achievement of an agreement with the Palestinians and security for Israelis."

Peace Now could not have known that Channel 1 TV would air an objective documentary tonight in the Real Story series focusing on Jews living in outposts in YESHA (Judea, Samaria and Gaza). The unnarrated film was made by avowed leftist Michal Kafra who neatly breaks many of the stereotypes of the "settlers."

Kafra trains her camera on several older Russian immigrants living in various outposts. There's only one American, but a number of idealistic, newly religious Sabras invite Kafra in for a sustained look at their log-cabin-like abode on a wind-blown hilltop in Samaria.

The footage is interspersed with news clips from the recent riots. It is deeply disturbing to view the program with the knowledge of today's attacks on Jews living in much larger Jewish villages. How will these tiny bands of Zionist pioneers be protected?

For Moshe Vogel, an Israeli government spokesman, the question of protection is turned on its head. Vogel tries to deflect the hostile questioning of foreign journalists at a news conference today. One young blond woman at the back of the sparsely populated briefing room aggressively asks Vogel why the IDF doesn't use water cannons to disperse "demonstrators." Vogel does not explain that the child rioters are merely the first line of attack, backed up by Tanzim terrorists armed with Kalashnikovs and M-16s. Instead, he politely tells her that there are just too many riots going on at once and H_2O is not a practical solution.

Despite the fact that the press briefing took place before the killings today, Vogel nevertheless acknowledged that "this is not a civilian uprising. This is low-intensity warfare."

Indeed, other official security bodies seem to have come to the same conclusion, since just this week, red and white signs appeared in many Jerusalem neighborhoods pointing to the location of the closest underground shelter. While all new construction in Israel must have a sealed, protected room in every apartment, many older buildings (mine included) have none.

Other signs plastered all over town announce the 10th anniversary of the murder of Rabbi Meir Kahane, who was gunned down in New York City. "Kahane was Right," declare the stark black and white banners.

Meanwhile, outside the prime minister's residence, Likud MK Limor Livnat continues her sit-in at a protest tent. People who are joining her effort are not the usual right wing crowd. There's a group from a high tech company in Raanana, as well as people from Gilo. Tonight, because of the new terror victims, Livnat is joined early in the evening by a vocal group of young religious students who light torches and stand across the street chanting, "Ehud, Go Home." Their voices amplified by megaphones echo through the neighborhood all the way down to the Jerusalem Theater. Meanwhile, Barak is in Chicago addressing the General Assembly of the United Jewish Communities.

As the evening wears on, car loads of angry YESHA residents begin to arrive at the tent from Neve Tzuf, home of the young mother killed today, and from nearby Ofra to protest the policies they believe led to today's tragedies.

No one is quite sure where the escalation is heading — but in the face of the outside threat, Israelis are closing ranks and bracing for the worst.

Enough!

Jerusalem, November 14, 2000   Word spread quickly...even as the victims of yesterday's murders were being buried, hammers pounded stakes into the ground to build protest tents across from the prime minister's office, and printing presses rolled to run off posters announcing a demonstration tonight with the theme, "Let the IDF Win."

The tents violate the grounds of one of Jerusalem's most beautiful parks, the Wohl Rose Garden, which lies between the Knesset and Kiryat Hamemshala, the area of large boxy government buildings not far from Hebrew University's Givat Ram campus. On this sunny, pleasant November afternoon, the park is fragrant with roses and manicured grass. If we were living in normal times in a normal place, this urban oasis would be peopled by strolling couples and families frolicking with their kids, but today the outer edge of the park has been turned into a harsh reminder of the nightmare of our violent society.

Grim-faced young volunteers prepare the tents with tables, banners and flags. Some of the girls are students of Sarah Leisha, the gym teacher who was murdered yesterday.

Each tent is designated for a different bloc of Jewish communities in YESHA. The Sanican toilets are wheeled into place and one patch of grass is strewn with sleeping bags. These protestors are in for the long haul. Prior to yesterday's killings the activists had already announced a mass demonstration next Wednesday in Jerusalem. But today, they handed out flyers calling on concerned Israelis to turn out at Zion Square in the middle of town tonight to call on Prime Minister Barak to "fight against the murderers."

It seems clear to everyone that the nature of the conflict has changed over the past 24 hours. While the rock throwers still come out on cue every day at certain junctions, the targets of Arafat's minions are now Jewish civilians traveling the roads of YESHA and the IDF soldiers who protect us all. It's guerilla warfare in the form of snipers who shoot with impunity at buses and cars from areas under Palestinian civil and security control. So far the IDF has strict orders not to pursue the terrorists. They confine their reaction to lobbing missiles at empty buildings — yesterday the Jericho casino took a few good hits from our army.

These shooting attacks are far more difficult to capture on camera, so dozens of TV crews are now out looking for stories. As I cross the street to leave the park, an NBC camera crew pulls up in its white jeep to check out the action at the protest tents. The sun is low in the sky, and the anchorman calls out to his assistant: "Line up the spokesman. Have him face the sun — I want him to squint."

I jump on a bus heading south. The sunset is spectacular in its dark pink and red hues which color the sky over Malcha, the hill next to Gilo, our border battle line. The driver has the radio tuned to the news channel. It has become almost unbearable to listen to the constant barrage of news and analysis. None of the politicians or academics has anything new or constructive to say, and for those of us in the relative safety of the cities, we have become quite inured to the rundown of places where attacks are currently taking place. It's almost like the traffic report — shooting at Junction X, stone throwing on road Y...

I head down to the rally at Kikar Tzion. About a thousand people turn up for the impromptu event. Hastily made hand-drawn signs with anti-Barak slogans are everywhere. Particularly poignant are the banners held by groups of teenage girls which read: "My teacher was murdered yesterday." The press swarm like bees to a couple of small kids carrying signs with pictures of the infamous Ramallah lyncher with blood on his hands. The caption: "Barak's Partner?"

The older teenage boys take over the square and form a large circle to dance and sing the well known anthem: "The whole world is a very narrow bridge. And the main thing is to have no fear at all."

121

Well known Kach members circulate amongst the crowd, passing out leaflets about the upcoming yahrzeit of Rabbi Meir Kahane. Well known rabbis are amongst the crowd too — I see Rabbi Eliezer Waldman from Kiryat Arba and Rav Ariel from Beit El.

The proceedings start with the recitation of Kel Moleh Rachamim, the prayer for the dead. At the point where the names of the deceased are mentioned, Rav Ariel inserts: "Those who died as martyrs at the hands of the sons of Ishmael in the Holy Land.." Next to me, a father hugs his sobbing teenage daughter, who mourns her teacher from Neve Tzuf.

A small fracas breaks out as a tiny group of three or four demonstrators screams out, "Death to Arabs," at the end of the prayer. They are shouted down by a couple of older men in knitted kippot.

Speaker after speaker has the same message — let the IDF do what we all know it is capable of doing. Go after the murderers. We have too many dead already. We're in a war, so let's demolish the enemy.

Between speakers, the crowd yells, "Go home, Ehud." Youngsters lead a spirited singing of Am Yisrael Chai — the People of Israel Lives.

The shopkeepers around the square are happy to finally have some business. The crowd disperses fairly early, and it's easy to see who's there from outside Jerusalem. They're the ones with guns slung over their backs, hurrying to their bullet-proof buses and cars to run the gauntlet of the shooting attacks on the way home.

A Day in the Life....

How does a regular day begin in the life of a normal family? The kids get ready for school, wave good-bye to their parents, hop on the school bus and arrive at school ready to greet their teachers and start the day, right?

Today, that mundane scenario was so hideously distorted that by 7:30 a.m. two teachers lay dead, five kids were seriously wounded, and their school bus was destroyed by a 122 mm. mortar.

Arab terrorists targeted the bus that left Kfar Darom in Gush Katif carrying 30 school kids and their teachers. The carnage was devastating. The bus was bullet-proof, preventing a larger number of casualties, but there's little defense against the kind of shells that had been routinely used to bomb targets in Lebanon.

The forty families who live behind the walls of Kfar Darom are in constant fear of just the kind of tragedy that occurred today. But the sight of their dead friends and wounded children sent them out to the streets beyond the concrete barriers this morning to protest the conditions which they believe led to today's horror.

Israel radio carries continuous commentary on the tragedy all morning. A rabbi from Gush Katif quietly notes that "Barak needs to know that this attack is not related to Gush Katif or any other place. It's just an attack against Jews," he says. His words echo the thoughts of the father of a critically injured IDF soldier who was interviewed yesterday, just hours before his 21 year old son would die. He was asked if he was upset that his son was serving in Gush Katif. Glaring at the interviewer, the middle aged man replied, "My son was protecting Jews. If it wasn't for Gush Katif, the terrorists would be in Ashkelon."

In reaction to the school bus bombing, dozens of Jerusalemites stop traffic at the entrance to the city this morning. Eventually they are forcibly removed, but many police officers offer sympathetic words to the demonstrators. By 2 p.m. hundreds gather outside Prime Minister Barak's Rehavia residence. Among them are relatives of Sara Leisha, the 42-year-old teacher from Neve Tzuf murdered just last week.

While Barak convenes an emergency cabinet session, Deputy Defense Minister Ephraim Sneh addresses a news conference at the press center. Sneh lays the blame for this morning's attack on Yasser Arafat. "It was a strategic terror attack whose purpose was to inflict irreversible damage to future Israeli-Palestinian negotiations or reconciliation," he declares.

I ask about his reaction to the anti-government demonstrations and the accusation of the Gush Katif residents who placed a sign on the burnt out shell of the school bus, saying: "Barak you have blood on your hands."

Sneh responds that the government's job is to pursue its objectives and not to react to the national mood. Once again he speaks of the Barak administration's fear of being judged by the rest of the world. "Our policy is not to fall into the trap to hit innocent (Arab) civilians and then to be accused by the international community," he says. In other words, Israeli strategic policy is dictated by the UN, Bill Clinton, the European Union and CNN.

Despite this morning's violence, which he attributes to Arafat, Sneh reiterates the position that the strategic goal of the Barak administration is to sign an agreement. "But we'll have to resume talks to achieve it, and that we can't do while the violence goes on."

Sneh is cagey about mentioning what kind of retaliation might be expected, but by the time darkness falls, we don't have to guess. Without warning, helicopter gunships start firing a barrage of missiles into military targets in Gaza. Electricity goes down, Fatah buildings and security offices close to Arafat's headquarters are destroyed.

The whole event is carried live on the two major Israeli TV channels. Channel One uses the official PA TV footage. It's a little eerie to be sitting in Jerusalem watching the bombing of Gaza with Arabic commentary.

While the attacks go on, a few thousand people gather in front of the prime minister's residence. Police and IDF block off Azza Street, and the predominantly national religious crowd faces the hastily constructed stage, waving Israeli flags and carrying wax torches that illuminate their strained faces. A few young girls sit at the curb, heads in their hands. Other, older protesters stand quietly, hands in their pockets, not quite knowing how to express their grief.

Photos of Arafat with "Murderer" printed in large red letters are peppered through the crowd. One huge home-made sign reads: "Ramat Aviv: Arafat won't forget you!"

Almost half the crowd are teenagers happy to provide the numerous cameramen with active footage. They climb onto each other's shoulders and chant: "Ehud Go Back Home.." As speaker after speaker mounts the stage to address the crowd, some get restive. One group of twenty-year-olds starts to yell: "Instead of talk, let's do something!"

Although there are no English-language signs — a fact noted by the roving eyes of several photographers who search in vain for something their readers will understand — one speaker addresses the crowd in English. It's Yehudit Gross, mother of Aharon Gross, an 18-year-old yeshiva student murdered by terrorists 18 years ago. Gross becomes increasingly strident as she speaks, and the cameras lap it up. Her closing comment is, "It's all dirty lies!" Her tone has whipped up the demonstrators a bit and a few start to yell, "Barak, Traitor," but they're quickly shouted down by others around them.

By 8:45 p.m things wind down — many have been at the site since 5 p.m. Hatikva, Psalms for the wounded, and a quick Ma'ariv (evening) prayer bring a close to this awful day — a day which should have ended with kids in Kfar Darom eating dinner, doing homework and refusing to go to bed....

On the Edge

Jerusalem, November 22, 2000   Hadera lies well within the Green Line, a few miles south of the ritzy villas and golf course of Caesarea. It's a fairly non-descript town with a large industrial area and a few large shopping malls. But its proximity to Area A, the area under complete PA civil and security control, is what has given Hadera name recognition in recent years.

Today, a remote control car bomb went off in Hadera's main street during the afternoon rush hour. Two Israelis died and 55 were injured in the blast. Earlier this year a much smaller bomb detonated in a garbage can in the town causing some injuries, but it was in April 1994, nine months after the Oslo agreement was signed, that a powerful device exploded at the Hadera bus station, claiming five lives. The blast was the first in a series of terror attacks that continued until 1997.

Today's horror unfolded before a nation still struggling to come to terms with the vicious assault on a bus carrying 30 kids to school two days ago. Three young children lie in a Beersheva Hospital with amputated limbs; a teacher and a maintenance worker were buried.

Now 57 more families, in what was commonly thought to be an undisputed area of the country, face the task of recovering the fragments of their lives.

Reaction here was swift. Prime Minister/Defense Minister Ehud Barak placed the blame on Yasser Arafat, who ordered the release of Hamas and Islamic Jihad terrorists. Barak promised that those responsible for the attack would be tracked down by the long arm of the IDF and Israeli security forces.

The left wing Peace Now organization condemned the bombing. Prof. Galia Golan, a prominent Peace Now spokesperson, said: "Violence and bloodshed only produce more violence and bloodshed. Such a tragic spiral underlines the imperative need to end the violence and return to the negotiating table."

Finance Minister Binyamin Ben-Eliezer, in a breaking voice, condemned the "barbaric" attack. He added that he cannot tolerate the "ritual" any longer. Ben-Eliezer was referring to the PA's routine denial of any involvement with such actions.

In standard terrorist doublespeak, a spokesman for the Hamas terror organization states that the blast was a natural reaction to continuing IDF aggression and the attack at Morag on Wednesday morning, in which several terrorists were killed by IDF soldiers. As if Hamas needed an excuse to perpetrate their violence!

Journalist Michael Widlanski, monitoring the official PA media tonight, reports that the Palestine Broadcast Company airs Yasser Arafat calling for continued Intifada violence. According to Widlanski, there are no condemnations of the attacks by Arafat, nor from any other PA official. Arafat's English language representatives appear on CNN and the BBC, however, providing sweeping condemnations for foreign and Israeli consumption. They place the blame for the latest violence outside the PA.

Meantime, Barak convenes an emergency meeting of the Security Cabinet, while 100,000 people gather in Kikar Tzion, Jerusalem's main square, under the banner: 'Let the IDF Win.'

The event, planned in reaction to the earlier killings, brings busloads of Israelis from towns and villages all over Israel to the capital. King George Street is a parking lot, filled with buses from Ashkelon, Petach Tikva, Rehovot, Kfar Saba, Beit Shemesh etc. A special effort was made to bring people from the "safe" areas of the country, since residents of Judea, Samaria and Gaza are prevented from traveling the roads at night. The roads are either closed by the IDF, or if they're open, shootings and stonings are now a routine occurrence.

The crowd stretches from Kikar Tzion almost to Machane Yehudah on Jaffa Street and covers the entire length of the Ben Yehuda Street pedestrian mall. Teenagers have virtually taken over the mall, some sitting on the ground singing and playing guitars, others greeting their friends and plastering their T shirts with anti-government bumper stickers. The place has the air of a giant youth group meeting.

The rally starts promptly at 7 p.m., with a live broadcast of the hourly news resonating through the square. The numbers of dead and wounded in Hadera are announced, and 100,000 people observe a moment of silence for the latest victims of the violence.

One speaker stands out among the usual array of right of center politicians who address the crowd. He is Ariel Difani, the 11-year-old son of one of the women injured in the Kfar Darom bus tragedy. He penned his words at his mother's bedside today. Climbing to the podium, the dark-haired boy wearing a colorful kippa defiantly tells Arafat he'd better forget about ever gaining control of Kfar Darom. It's my home, it's Jewish land, and no one is ever going to take that away from me, Ariel declares. We've already paid a heavy price, he continues. The serious words sound incongruous coming from this young boy who, in normal times in a normal place, would be home playing computer games.

Tuning into the news at the conclusion of the demonstration, we hear Dr. Meir Oren of Hadera's Hillel Yaffe Hospital explain that victims continue to make their way to the hospital. Many people went home from the site of the blast but then experienced a delayed physical or psychological reaction to the situation. Dr. Oren says he expects to see a steady flow of patients arriving at the emergency room during the night.

Finally we learn the identity of the victims: Shoshana Reiss, 20, of Hadera and Meir Barami, 35, of Givat Olga. Meir, divorced, leaves behind three children, a 7-year-old daughter and 5-year-old twins.

The close of another day in a country on edge.

Celebrating the Zionist Festival

Jerusalem, November 27, 2000   Israel's rabbis designated last Monday as Yom Kippur Katan — a special half day of fasting and prayer — in response to our worsening security situation. But for Jews from Ethiopia the 29th of Cheshvan has long been observed as a fast day, followed by a festive meal, in honor of the festival of Segd.

Dozens of kessim (Ethiopian Jewish religious leaders) make their way to the Western Wall to celebrate the day which expresses their yearning for Zion and their gratitude for the Torah. The slender figures cut an elegant path through the plaza in front of the wall. Swathed in simple white robes, tallits draped over their narrow shoulders, the kessim are accompanied by an entourage which includes an escort holding a colorful umbrella over their heads. The Ethiopian women arrive separately, clothed in their distinctive white dresses adorned with colorful hand-embroidered trim. Shoulders cloaked in white shawls, heads covered with colorful head scarves, the women advance shyly toward the Kotel to take part in the prayer service marking Segd here in the holy city.

Prior to their mass aliya, generations of Ethiopian Jews yearned for Zion and expressed their longing in the annual Segd festival. Jews would walk for days to arrive at a mountain top, where thousands would join in prayer and listen to Torah readings. Following the afternoon prayers and the blowing of the shofar, the community would descend from the mountain to partake of a festive meal. The holiday has its origins in the time of the prophet Nehemia, when the entire Jewish community assembled in Jerusalem for a day of fasting and confession. The day also commemorates the covenant between God and the Jewish people at Mt. Sinai.

For many young Ethiopian Jews now living in Israel, the

mountain top Segd exists only as a story recounted by their parents. They fled Ethiopia too young to have taken part in the unique festival there. But this year one prominent Jerusalem educational institution made sure that Segd got the attention it deserves amongst the younger generation.

Nishmat, the Jerusalem Center for Advanced Jewish Study for Women based in Bayit Vegan, recently celebrated an observance of Segd that wove together tradition, culture, respect, education, song and prayer.

Fifteen young Ethiopian Jewish women are enrolled at Nishmat this year in an inaugural college preparatory program. They study secular subjects to prepare themselves for the tough college entrance exams, as well as a full load of Judaic studies offered by the innovative Nishmat curriculum.

The women share dormitory space with native Israeli and English-speaking students, to promote social integration. Several English speakers note that the Ethiopian women are generally shy and reserved, but tonight they proudly show off their remarkable culture.

After the recitation of Psalms led by an Israeli student, Zahava, a slight, Ethiopian young woman with long, dark hair and delicate features, opens the evening. All the Ethiopian students present are dressed in the clothing unique to their community. Zahava wears a sleek, white embroidered dress, but she calls up Shlomit, dressed in a more conservative, billowy robe, to point out the difference between the kind of clothing their mothers and grandmothers wear and their own more up to date, but still traditional garb.

The women carry themselves gracefully and naturally in the robes, their heads covered with filmy white shawls. Zahava brings out an array of traditional hand-made colorful basketware from a display table at the side of the room, carefully describing how each one is made and used.

As she speaks, a diminutive man, with a silver beard and wearing a knitted kippa, enters the room. The students all rise to acknowledge the arrival of Rabbi David Yosef, a kes of the Ethiopian community. Rabbi Yosef was invited to give the Israeli and English-speaking students a presentation on the origins of Segd. His lively eyes sparkle and quick smiles flit across his face as he lets the women in on his extraordinary life story, in order for them to understand where Segd fits into the life of the Ethiopian Jew.

Rav Yosef graphically describes how men and women would separately observe the ritual of ascending the mountain for the great Segd gathering. He points out that the tradition of Segd was handed down orally from generation to generation. "Many Jews believe that we didn't know of the Oral Law," he says. Rav Yosef carefully explains the Ethiopian Jewish engagement and wedding ceremonies and asserts that their practice conforms to the Mishnaic description in Tractate Kiddushin (part of the Oral Law) of what constitutes proper Jewish betrothal.

He closes his remarks by noting that Segd was essentially a way of remembering Jerusalem and strengthening Jews in a difficult galut (Diaspora) situation. But the holiday is just as relevant today. "We yearned for Jerusalem for thousands of years," Rav Yosef notes. "Today, in Jerusalem, we celebrate...but just as we say 'Next year in Jerusalem' at the Passover seder, so, too, at Segd we pray for a rebuilt Jerusalem."

Rav Yosef takes the Ethiopian students aside for five minutes while the other women put the finishing touches to the special Ethiopian meal they have prepared. Platters of injara, the Ethiopian pita bread, are laid out along with an assortment of dairy items and cooked and raw vegetables, served by the young Ethiopian women.

Nishmat's founder and dean, the dynamic Rabbanit Chana Henkin, addresses the group while everyone munches on the delicacies. Henkin, her eyes glowing with pride at the self-assuredness of her students, speaks from the heart as she tells the women how she is moved at the sight of a new generation of immigrants from an ancient Jewish community perpetuating the observance of a unique festival. Rav Yosef's vivid description of

Jewish life in Ethiopia reminds her of a significant childhood experience. Henkin never met her paternal grandfather, but she recalls that once someone from his village came to visit and shared stories of her ancestors. "He provided a window into a world I would never have known, just like Rav Yosef did today," Henkin says.

Sara, the bespectacled eldest daughter of a kes in Ashdod, rises to teach the women some traditional Ethiopian songs in the Amharic language from a handwritten songbook compiled and printed by the students for the occasion. Most of the verses speak of Jerusalem. Accompanied by the guitar of one of the Israelis, the spirited singing virtually drowns out the loud booms of the mortar shell volleys in Gilo just across the valley.

For Ziva, a shy twenty-year-old from Ashkelon with dark braided hair, the Segd celebration at Nishmat was a significant milestone. "This was a moment to tell our story," she said quietly. "I feel like it's a day of unity for us." For the young woman who arrived in Israel with her parents twelve years ago, the observance of the ancient holiday serves as a reminder that "there's so much to remember...."

Rabbanit Chana Henkin and Sara Neima, Nishmat student.

The Spirit of the People

Jerusalem, December 6, 2000   The violence that has now dragged on for more than two months, and which permeates almost every sector of our lives, has in fact caused one or two positive shifts in Israeli society. The most obvious is a closing of the ranks — a sense that, despite the political wrangling, we're all still family.

Golan residents volunteer their services to help protect the roads for their endangered Jordan Valley brethren; Jordan Valley bus drivers trade shifts with their Gush Katif counterparts, and the people from the south and Gilo are invited to Galilee kibbutz guest houses for a free weekend of relaxation.

These actions are but one manifestation of the spirit of the people of Israel. Since the outbreak of this crisis I've come into contact with people who exemplify that unique Israeli combination of strength and goodness which many thought had been long buried under materialism and individualism.

Take Haggai, for example. Haggai drove me to a conference in Sderot the other day. He's a father of five kids who holds down two jobs. He picked me up in his blue minivan which he uses to transport kids to school from his community of Alon Shvut in Gush Etzion just south of Jerusalem. In the middle of the day, when he's not with the kids, Haggai takes off for the film studios of Neve Ilan where he works as a technician.

Haggai is in his forties, with dark disheveled hair, a shaggy mustache, and a knitted kipa which looks like it's about to slide off the side of his head at any moment. Our conversation quickly turns to "the situation." Haggai tells me quietly that he grew up in Kfar Maimon, a small moshav in the south. He doesn't need to tell me that the village was home to a recent terror victim. Ayelet Hashahar Levy, 24, the daughter of National Religious Party leader Rabbi

Yitzhak Levy, who also spent her early years at Kfar Maimon. Haggai recounts his shiva visit to the Levy family back at his birthplace.

Amongst the dozens of people there, Haggai found himself sitting next to another old friend from his Kfar Maimon days, Noga Cohen. Noga now lives in Kfar Darom, and he hadn't seen her for a while. They updated each other on their kid's latest escapades and went on their way.

Just three weeks later, Haggai was devastated to hear on the news that three of his old friend's kids were critically injured by the terrorist bomb which pierced a school bus in Kfar Darom, claiming the lives of two adults. All three children subsequently had limbs amputated and now lie in hospital. Haggai and his wife organize a constant stream of visitors to the family; they assisted in setting up a fund to help with expenses and they sit with the family at the hospital. Just plain acts of loving kindness ingrained in their character.

I get to ride home from the Sderot conference with another driver, Zion. Zion is older, a grandfather of nine. Zion's ancestors are Turkish Jews who lived in Iran before arriving in Israel in the 1940s. Zion decides to take me back via the scenic route — past Bet Guvrin and through the beautiful rolling hills of Emek Ha'ela, past the new towns of Tzur Hadassah and Beitar, and out to the tunnel road into Jerusalem. The roads are almost completely deserted, save for the occasional jeep. Zion is intimately familiar with this route as it goes by his rural home of Neve Michael. As we pass each site along the way, Zion tells me stories of the founders and of the people who live there now. His passionate love for the land comes through in his every word. He relates how he wakes up early each morning and putters in his garden before enjoying a cup of coffee with his wife. He marvels at the beauty of the land he has helped cultivate.

Zion explains how his community of 150 families works. "We visit each other all the time. No one comes to visit without something from the orchards or fields in his hands," he says. Bushels of grapes, avocados, oranges — whatever happens to be in season is shared by the families of Neve Michael. With a broad smile he describes his ultimate joy — Shabbat gatherings of his children and grandchildren. "You should see my daughter," says Zion. "She can't do enough for us. She won't let my wife do a thing in the kitchen while she's there. Ach...what a pleasure." Just a simple, natural love of land and family ingrained in his character.

Israelis living in Judea and Samaria are passionate about the land too, but their feelings these days have an urgent edge to them. One day last week I accompanied Minister for Diaspora Affairs Michael Melchior on a visit to the embattled communities of Psagot and Eli. Melchior, a leader of Meimad, the left wing religious party, decided that he needed to reassure people in those small settlements that, despite their political differences, he and his party stood with them in these terrible times.

The impetus for the visit was the publication of an open letter, signed by Peace Now, calling for the dismantling of settlements. The fringe group chose to run the ads not only in Israeli papers, but also in a Palestinian daily published in Ramallah. Melchior is outraged at the action which he feels legitimizes and encourages violence against Jews living in YESHA.

At Eli, a hilltop community of some 3,000 people, Melchior asks for a meeting with the students and faculty of Yeshivat Bnai David, a pre-army yeshiva program. The discussion is closed to the press, but we are briefed by Gidon Prager while the ministerial meeting takes place. Gidon is young, tall and clean shaven. His cardigan sweater and owlish glasses give him a scholarly look. He addresses the journalists in perfect English learned from his British-born parents.

Gidon speaks calmly about the high tech company he's founded in Eli. He tells us about the security concerns of the people of Eli and neighboring communities. Gidon fields some hostile questions with measured responses, quietly explaining his point of view. He is self-assured without being arrogant and refuses to be lured into the journalists lair. He firmly but respectfully reiterates his opinion that the residents of Eli will not be frightened into violent responses to Arab terror, and repeatedly asserts that any change in the situation will come about only through democratic means. Just a rational, firm belief in the justness of Israel's claims ingrained in his character.

Minister Melchior is invited to the community center for a meeting with Eli community leaders. It's an earnest, thoughtful and unsettling discussion. The bearded Eli representatives lay out their feelings about the government's attitude toward the settlements. The men wear the knitted kippot of the national religious movement. Their furrowed brows reveal their concern and consternation. "We're brothers," says one of the men to Minister Melchior. "We must always remember we're brothers...but you have to agree that what the Arabs are doing in trying to steal away our country is a crime," he continues. He passionately argues that the left must be more careful with language. "If we all buy into the argument that we're a 'foreign occupying government' here, there's no hope," he says. Rabbi Eli Sadan speaks up: "We have to keep our faith...we won't accept the Arab attempts to rewrite history and deny our historic claims here." Rabbi Sadan fervently urges Melchior to exert his influence on the secular leftist politicians. "Your words (that some settlements will have to go) have created a terrible dynamic," Sadan continues, accusing Melchior of undermining the morale in the small outlying communities. Just a passionate, total commitment to Zionism ingrained in his character.

The compassion of some Israelis is inspiring. Twenty-seven-year old Keren Leibovich won three gold medals in swimming at the Sydney Paralympic Games. Leibovitch, disabled since 1992 from an accident during her army service, made it her business to travel down to Soroka Hospital in Beersheva to pay a special visit to the three young Cohen children, who will spend the rest of their lives missing one or two limbs as a result of the Kfar Darom terror attack.

Keren wants to show the children that the challenges of physical disability can be overcome — to give them hope for a productive future. Just empathetic caring and compassion ingrained in her character.

My doorbell rings. Standing smiling at the threshold are two long-haired, twenty-something young men in blue youth movement shirts. They're holding bulging plastic bags and ask if I have any candy to contribute to their collection for distribution to hospitalized kids. The Israeli version of trick or treat. Just a sense of responsibility and a natural impulse to care for others ingrained in their character.

It's not only native Israelis who exemplify these characteristics. I spent a Shabbat filled with humor, concern and spirit at the home of Avi and Barbara Grant in Ra'anana. The Grants, immigrants from England, in Israel just five years this time around, Avi and Barbara are on the front lines of the battle for media balance. Avi is a retired engineer. Congenial and intelligent, Avi has a wealth of knowledge and life experience, which he puts to good use writing and circulating letters to papers all over the world advocating Israel's interests. Barbara is a PR professional who understands the workings of the media world. She's articulate and assertive, and relentless in her pursuit of fairness from the press. Since the start of the violence, Barbara has found her days consumed with advocating Israel's case by phone, fax and e-mail. Her business has suffered, but every day she comes up with fresh ideas for engaging journalists in lively discussion and politely challenges their ignorance and willful bias. Just a total commitment to the pursuit of truth ingrained in her character.

Every few weeks I spend a spirited Friday night with the Cohn family in Jerusalem's Kiryat Shmuel neighborhood. There are hundreds of us who count ourselves among the fortunate targets of Moshe and Ruth Cohn's hospitality. The lively couple, who emigrated from London five years ago to join their children here, welcome dozens of guests to their Shabbat table every week. It's always an eclectic group of immigrants and native-born Israelis; young and old; singles and couples. Many long-term friendships have been forged around that table, between people who might otherwise never have met. When I ask Moshe if I may reciprocate one Shabbat, he politely declines, informing me in his London accent: "There are too many interesting people around that WE still have to invite." Just a genuine desire ingrained in his character to spread friendship and warmth and fulfill the mitzvah of welcoming guests.

The list could go on — performers like Yehuda Glantz, originally from South America, who almost stopped the show at the opening of the recent Jerusalem Du Siach (dialogue) Festival. Glantz, a Hasidic/rock/world beat singer and musician with a bushy black beard, long twirly sidelocks and a powerful stage presence, joined forces with Gidi Gov, the quintessential secular sabra singer, to sing 'Kol Haolam Kulo, Gesher Tzar Meod.' (The whole world is a very narrow bridge.) The chorus, belted out by the two performers on stage as well as everyone in the packed auditorium, is: "But the main thing above all, is not to be afraid at all."

Surrounded here by people such as those I've described, it's a lot easier to internalize that mantra. The spirit of the people of Israel is battered, but alive and well.

Kol Yisrael Areivin, Zeh BaZeh
(All Jews are Responsible For One Another)

Israel, January 1, 2001   Despite snowstorms which closed New York area airports, a delegation of sixteen people accompanying Rabbi Avi Weiss, the national president of the Coalition for Jewish Concerns-Amcha, arrived in Israel yesterday evening.

From the airport, the group traveled directly to the Kotel, followed by a meal at the unique Between The Arches Restaurant, hollowed out of a Crusader period arch in the Old City.

Today the itinerary included an extensive tour of Jewish communities in Hebron; a look at the historic Jewish cemetery in the city; a visit to the Avraham Avinu synagogue and a look at its 700-year-old sefer Torah; tfilla (prayers) at the Cave of the Patriarchs and a moving encounter with Chaim Didovsky, husband of murdered teacher Rina Didovsky.

For Didovsky, left to raise his six children alone, it was the first time he had spoken publicly about his wife's murder three weeks ago. He described how his family sat down to the Friday night meal on the day of Rina's funeral. "We ate the food she herself had prepared that morning," Chaim told the group, with tears in his eyes. Their 18-month-old son has just started to walk, "but his mother will never see him...."

Kiryat Arba educational institutions were the next stop for the group — Rabbi Eliezer Waldman, Rosh Yeshiva of Yeshivat Nir, hosted the New York guests. A quick visit to the Ulpana (Girl's High School), where 500 young women are living and learning, gave the group an opportunity to meet the next generation of committed Jews.

Rabbi Shlomo Riskin and his wife Vicki escorted the visitors to

Rabbi Avi Weiss speaks to the press at a new Jewish outpost.

Givat Dagan, a proposed new Efrat neighborhood bordering on Bethlehem. As the sun set over the stark beauty of the Judean Hills, Rabbi Riskin enthusiastically pointed out the spot where new families would shortly be joining the Efrat community. Walking past the pre-fab buildings of the yeshiva, Rabbi Riskin showed us the concrete slabs placed by the IDF to protect the hill from the regular Arab shooting attacks.

A chance encounter with a lone IDF tank officer stationed on the hill soon turned into a Jewish geography session. The young man, from a prominent Brooklyn family, is completing the second year of his army service. He made aliya, while his parents remain in New York.

During the course of the day, the group delivered toys to the children of needy Hebron families, and Rabbi Weiss presented Chaim Didovsky with a significant contribution to the Didovsky Fund which will help support his six children.

A sad opportunity to fulfill the obligation to take responsibility for a fellow Jew.

Yerushalayim B'sakana
(Jerusalem in Danger)

Jerusalem, January 2, 2001   After a few days of visits with bereaved families of terror victims in small communities in YESHA, Rabbi Weiss's group focused today on Jerusalem. Traveling a brief 10 minutes from the center of the city, we arrive at the Gilo junction to transfer from our mini-bus to an armored shuttle bus, which will take us the last two minutes across the checkpoint to the Israeli enclave of Rachel's Tomb within PA-controlled Bethlehem.

Dozens of Arabs walk past us as we wait in the slow drizzle for the 9 a.m. bus to arrive. These local residents don't need bullet-proof vehicles to go back and forth from Bethlehem.

Waiting for the bus, we have a clear view of the construction at Har Homa, Jerusalem's newest eastern neighborhood just across the valley. A platoon of soldiers passes by in a heavily armored personnel carrier that looks like it could withstand a nuclear blast.

At the kever, we're told to alight from the bus only by the front door, which lets out directly into the fortified structure built around the site a couple of years ago. We spend half an hour in prayer before catching the same bus back to the junction after it disgorges another load of passengers.

We pass the Kever Rachel tent at the entrance to the tunnel roads. The place is manned 24 hours a day by a group of determined women from Hebron, Jerusalem and Efrat, who have pledged not to leave until free access to Kever Rachel is restored.

A short tour of Gilo's fortifications before we meet Uri Bank on Rechov Ha'anafa, the street facing the Beit Jala shooting gallery. Uri is a leader of the Gilo Residents Council who has lived in the neighborhood for 19 years. It's been quiet in recent days, so we don't even bother to stand behind the concrete barricades designed to protect against the snipers from across the valley.

Uri explains the consternation of Gilo residents and the effect the shellings have had on people's lives. Since Christmas, the area has been relatively peaceful, but there's nothing to prevent a renewed flare-up across the picturesque valley. We look up at the sandbagged windows facing Beit Jala as Uri points out that only miracles can explain how only two Israelis have been seriously injured in the violence.

Leaving Gilo, we take a five-minute ride to the Tayelet, or Haas Promenade, in Talpiot, a place of unparalleled vistas over the Old City and eastern Jerusalem. From here it is easy to see the prominent newly constructed building in Abu Dis which Arafat has designated for his capital. Abu Dis backs directly onto the Mount of Olives cemetery which faces Har Habayit, the Temple Mount — under the Clinton/Barak chopping block.

It's amazing to see that the entire eastern part of the city — the very places which have the most historic, spiritual and religious significance for Jews — has been largely undeveloped by every Israeli government since 1967. Only in the past few years have small areas of private Jewish development been initiated in an attempt to establish a Jewish foothold there.

One of these is the old/new Shimon HaTzaddik neighborhood in the area commonly known as Sheikh Jarrah, just north of the Old City, to the east of Meah Shearim. Here, students from Yeshivat Beit Orot have worked quietly to revitalize an area which was established as a Jewish neighborhood in the late 1890s.

Passing through the Mount Scopus campus of Hebrew University, we arrive at Yeshivat Beit Orot, the only living Jewish presence on the Mount of Olives. The yeshiva was founded 10 years ago by Rav Benny Elon and Hanan Porat and now educates 100 students who serve in the IDF, along with their yeshiva studies.

Chaim Silberstein, Beit Orot executive director, gives us a detailed rundown of the security situation on the Mount of Olives, as well as an extensive overview of how Clinton's proposal will endanger Jewish Jerusalem.

We spend the afternoon on an intensive tour of the ancient City of David, just outside the southern walls of the Old City. Rabbi David Marcus, the energetic and knowledgeable development director, leads us through every facet of the remarkable area where Jerusalem was founded. The latest discoveries at Beit HaMayan in the Kidron Valley take our breath away, as layers of Jewish history peel away before our eyes.

In the evening we meet the parents of Binny Avraham, one of three Israeli soldiers kidnapped on the Lebanese border last October. The Avrahams are accompanied by Michael Landsberg, secretary general of the World Labour Zionist Movement, who is volunteering to help the family. Michael and the Avrahams describe their frustration at the Israeli government's lack of information regarding the missing soldiers. Chaim Avraham, a small, balding man with sad eyes sagging behind his glasses, explains quietly that Binny was named after Chaim's brother Benjamin who was killed in the 1973 Yom Kippur War. "That's how life is here," he says with a shrug.

We brainstorm on how communities in the States can help, and the Avrahams leave us with T-shirts, blue lapel ribbons and postcards. Rabbi Weiss, who has been active in the campaign for the "older" Israeli MIAs (Ron Arad, Zach Baumel, Yehuda Katz and Tzvi Feldman), lends his advice and hands the Avrahams a substantial check to help in their campaign.

Tomorrow it's on to the Gush Katif communities south of Gaza.

Heading South Again

Gush Katif, January 4, 2001   It's drizzling in Jerusalem as our bullet-proof bus pulls out of the hotel parking lot for the two-hour ride to the Kissufim junction at the entrance to Gush Katif.

The skies clear as we approach the point where we pick up our army escort for the short journey through PA-controlled territory from Kissufim to the Gefen checkpoint. This road, about two miles long, is the only access Israelis have to the Jewish communities of the Katif Bloc, south of Gaza. According to the Oslo Accords, the road is under Israeli security control, but the area to either side of it is PA country — hence the regular, deadly attacks which have taken place here in recent months.

Kissufim is abuzz with military personnel. Soldiers sit in heavily armed jeeps ready to accompany Israeli vehicles through the dangerous stretch of highway. Others maintain lookout posts over the adjacent territory, while dozens of IDF "jobniks" (non-combatant soldiers) work on maintaining the army vehicles lining the roadway.

We wait a few minutes while the commander radios ahead to Gefen to make sure all is clear, and then we are joined by Wahid (Rabbi Weiss calls him Wayne...), a tall, slim Druse soldier who tells our driver in staccato tones how to drive through the area. "You go no more than 60 km per hour; you follow the jeep in front of you at all times; whatever happens, you just keep following that jeep. Understood?" David, our driver, nods confidently and welcomes another soldier in full battle gear, who rides with us, while his colleagues bring up the rear in another jeep.

We set out at the appointed pace and ride uneventfully to Gefen. Taking leave of our escorts once we're in the relative safety of the Gush itself, we head for the small moshav of Netzer Hazani. Here we're met by Rabbi Chaim Schneid, a former classmate of Rabbi Weiss at Yeshiva University. Rabbi Schneid, or Chaim, as he prefers to be called, is an organic farmer at the moshav. He's been growing cherry tomatoes and other organic crops here for 23 years. A stocky man with greying beard and large knitted kipa, Chaim tells us about Netzer Hazani. 65 families from 18 countries make their home here. Fifty percent are Sephardic Jews, twenty five percent are of Yemenite origin, and twenty five percent are Ashkenazim.

Chaim maintains five dunams (about 3½ acres) of hothouses on the fence of the moshav. Since the latest outbreak of violence, he has not been officially allowed to go to work in the hothouses. Shooting goes on day and night. It's an economic disaster, he says, so he sneaks in to keep things going. Because things have been quiet today, he takes us into one of the hothouses, pointing out the large Arab house just across the fence which is the source of the shooting.

Inside, we stand on the plastic floor as Chaim explains how his farming conforms completely with shmitta (seventh year, when the land must lay fallow) law. He explains that his Arab workers have not been coming lately, even though most of them are desperate to earn a living and "they hate Arafat more than we do."

Before we leave Netzer Hazani, Chaim tells the group that one of the answers to the current situation is mass aliya from western countries. Rabbi Weiss asks his old classmate if the moshav has plans to relocate in the eventuality that the Barak proposal goes through. "We don't think about that," Chaim responds. "We're here, our home and livelihood are here, and that's that."

We have arranged to meet Rachel Gage at the gate to Neveh Dekalim, the largest community in the Gush. She is to take us to the newest settlement — Kfar Hayam, established after the bus bomb attack at Kfar Darom which claimed the lives of her friends Miriam Amitai and Gabi Biton. At the gate, Ayelet is there instead of Rachel. A beautiful, dark-haired, shy young woman — Ayelet explains that Rachel is busy at their new home dealing with the press. As we drive to Kfar Hayam, a few minutes in the direction of the sea, Ayelet explains the context of the tiny new settlement project. We pass down a one lane road lined with Arab houses on both sides. "They're Moasin," Ayelet notes — an Arab sect that is generally friendly to their Jewish neighbors. They moved in after the signing of the Oslo Accords of 1993.

Our group gets off the bus, stepping onto the fine white sand of the Kfar Hayam beach. The setting is idyllic — palm trees wave under the bright winter sun, and the bright blue of the Mediterranean sparkles about 50 yards away. A few pre-fab houses sit close to the road watched over by an IDF guardpost, but the main part of the new yishuv consists of 10 concrete structures. They are the abandoned summer homes of Egyptian army officers — dating back to pre-1967. Doorless and windowless, the buildings still display the remains of their ornate tile floors.

We're welcomed by Rachel and the other young couple who live at Kfar Hayam. They've set up a long table with light refreshments in one of the larger structures. We look out at the sea through a flapping Israeli flag which serves as their front door. Rachel, an engaging 22-year-old, explains in English how the houses were just hooked up to the electricity grid, but that they're still using chemical toilets.

As we talk, an Israel TV Channel 1 crew in flak jackets prowls around. Rachel is reluctant to talk with them for two reasons. Firstly, she feels that if the project is publicized before more families move in, it will be too easy for anti-settlement forces to move them out. Secondly, her parents have no idea she's living on the beach in Gush Katif, and she wants to break the news to them gently...

Rachel shows us through one of the sparsely furnished structures where she lives with Ayelet. Next door, a larger building has been set up as a synagogue. "We came here right after the terrorist incident at Kfar Darom," she says. "It was a way to channel our rage — to build a new synagogue and create a new place where Jews will live and pray. We feel that's constructive," she continued.

Their plans are to obtain official permits, then to knock down the old Egyptian structures and start to build a real Jewish community on the beach. "Anyone want to invest in the new Miami Beach?" asks one member of our group.

Lunch was waiting for us in the dining room of the girl's high school at Neve Dekalim. The bright, tidy new campus of the school just a few blocks from the beach seems to be an ideal setting — except for the nightly shelling. Rachel Saperstein, a long time American transplant to Neve Dekalim, tells us about the school while we enjoy lunch. Girls from all over Israel study there — the education is religious Zionist in orientation, and the school has an excellent reputation. She hands out copies of the newsletter produced by her English class. Almost every article is dedicated to the memory of Miriam Amitai, a beloved teacher killed a month earlier as she traveled to the school from her home in nearby Kfar Darom.

Miriam's husband Lazar stops by to meet us. A striking young man in his late thirties, with thick, dark hair and dark beard, Lazar is wearing a Big Apple-NY sweat shirt, with a gun slung over his shoulder.

Lazar tells us quietly what the loss of his wife has meant to his family. Their three daughters and one son, aged 14, 12, 11 and 10, have all taken it hard, but only the 10-year-old expresses the longing for her mother through tears. "The others are closed," he says.

Lazar accompanies us to his home village of Kfar Darom — a concrete fortified Jewish enclave in the midst of Arab neighbors. We go in with full military escort, and one of the soldiers stays on the bus while we walk around the village, accompanied by new immigrant Sara Freedman.

We stop first for a brief memorial ceremony where the American student from New Jersey, Alisa Flatow, was killed in a bus bomb attack a few years ago. A simple marker stands at the spot, and Alisa's name is inscribed together with seven or eight IDF soldiers who died in the same incident. Rabbi Weiss recites the Kel Moleh Rachamim prayer, and we observe a minute of silence together with Lazer Amitai — the monument is right outside his front door.

Sara, a young vibrant woman who made aliya from Miami, proudly shows us around her new home. A few of us break off to see if we can visit the widow of Gabi Biton, the 34-year-old who was killed in the bus bomb attack, leaving his wife and six children. The door to the simple Biton family home is open, but no one is there, so we leave the toys the group has bought from New York in the middle of the floor. It's difficult not to look at the family photos of the smiling Biton family which line the bookshelves.

There's so much to see at Kfar Darom — the hydroponic vegetable processing plant which provides bug-free produce to places all over the world, for example — but our army escorts are getting anxious as darkness begins to encroach, so we join the rest of the yishuv in the synagogue for mincha (afternoon service) and reluctantly climb onto the bus for the ride to the checkpoint and on back to Jerusalem.

Ayelet and Rachel, young pioneers at Kfar Hayam, Gush Katif.

Despite the grueling day, group members gather later in the evening to hear from Itamar Marcus, the director of Palestine Media Watch. Marcus, a former member of the Hebrew Institute of Riverdale, gives us an illustrated, up to the minute rundown of Arab incitement which his organization monitors closely. PMW hires former IDF intelligence officers who are fluent in Arabic to read official PA newspapers and watch hours of official Arab TV stations, in order to provide Israelis with an accurate picture of how Arafat is educating his public. The material is translated into Hebrew and English and is widely used as a barometer of Arafat's intentions.

Marcus, an Efrat resident, apologizes for leaving his cellphone open. His son is serving on the northern border and is expected home tonight for the first time in three weeks. Itamar doesn't want to miss the opportunity to connect with him for the drive home. Just before our meeting breaks up, young Yoav, a strapping, tall 18-year-old, arrives from the front. He's kind enough to answer a few questions before heading home with his father.

Our group dribbles quietly out of the room — the day has left us with plenty to think about.

The Shomron

Samaria, January 5, 2001 Today members of the CJC-Amcha solidarity visit to Israel learned about the Zionist response to terrorism.

In a day which begins with a visit to sandbagged Jewish homes in Psagot and a peek into the underground nerve center of the regional security service at the village bordering Ramallah, the U.S visitors witness the first full day of operations at an outpost set up overlooking the spot where Binyamin and Talia Kahane were murdered last Sunday.

Two large blue and white tents and a look-out tower topped by a large Israeli flag have been set up by residents of nearby Ofra as a response to the tragedy which left six young children orphans.

Today the site is buzzing with activity. A class of girls from the Ofra girls' high school is perched on plastic chairs on the rocky ground, listening to a lesson from their teacher. Further up the hill, the cameras roll as Ofra's rabbi, Avi Grisser, is interviewed by Israel's government TV channel. A bulldozer leveling more of the hill provides an interesting backdrop for the crew.

Likud MK Uzi Landau is there to lend support to the dozen or so young men in knitted kippot who busied themselves around the site. The arrival of our group of twenty people causes quite a stir. Two British newspaper reporters materialize out of nowhere to interview Rabbi Weiss. Site organizers are thrilled to receive moral support, and both Rav Grisser and MK Landau address the group, explaining that their efforts are intended to help safeguard the road for traveling residents of the nearby Jewish communities.

Both leaders called the current campaign a battle for Israel's soul. "The present government has given up on every principle we raised our kids on," said MK Landau, chairman of the Knesset

Foreign Affairs Committee. "Barak has no government, no support, yet he forces his policies on the people," Landau continues.

"We're being pushed into ghettos in our own country," he declares, before leaving to join hundreds of local residents on a march to Jerusalem.

Across the road we can clearly see the Arab village of Ein Yabroud, where the gunfire which killed the Kahanes originated. In the courtyard of a four story mansion, dozens of young Arabs gather to protest the IDF bulldozers which are demolishing a concrete wall in the field bordering the road. This rather pathetic action was intended to send a message to the murderers.

As we scramble back down the hill toward our waiting armored bus, we pass Alex and Yudit Gross bearing trays of cookies and cartons of soda for the new settlers. The Grosses have something in common with the Kahane family. Their 18-year-old son, Aharon, was gunned down in Hebron in 1983.

We travel on towards Shilo, a beautiful mountaintop community of 200 families, and home of our guide Era Rapaport. Mark Provisor, the security chief of the village, tells us his job is made more difficult because the IDF, on orders from the government, "isn't taking enough action."

Life goes on behind sandbagged windows in Psagot.

We share lunch with the lively students of the girls' high school in Maale Levona. One of their teachers, Sara Leisha, was another recent victim of the renewed Arab violence. She was gunned down as she was driving to Jerusalem with the school's executive director.

Before the girls go off for their afternoon classes, Rabbi Weiss pulls out his guitar and begins to sing a song with the chorus: "Kulanu k'echad b'or panecha..." "All of us, as one, in the light of Your presence." The girls jump up to dance right in front of the memorial corner they've created for their fallen teacher. Sara Leisha's picture smiles out from behind the glass case emblazoned with verses from the Eishet Chayil (Woman of Valor) poem.

Next stop is Eilon Moreh just outside PA-occupied Shechem (Nablus). We are here to leave a contribution for the widow and six children of Rabbi Hillel Lieberman. Rabbi Lieberman was murdered on the day the Arabs destroyed Joseph's Tomb. His father is a well-known congregational rabbi in Brooklyn. Yael Lieberman, a short, olive-complexioned young woman, gets onto the bus with one of her small children to thank us for coming. She brings with her a condolence letter written by Binyamin Kahane after Hillel's murder. Kahane speaks of turning bitter experiences into sweet ones, and his hope in the imminent arrival of the Messiah.

Eilon Moreh is home to several thriving educational institutions, as well as a high tech zone and a field school. The single family homes are spaced out on the hills and kids ride about freely on bikes and scooters. The views into Shechem over the ancient hills of Samaria are spectacular.

Traveling back to Jerusalem in the waning light of a wintry late afternoon, the group falls silent, with our bus driver mumbling to himself as he whips along the deserted roads, flying though the Arab villages along the way.

The Invincible Jerusalem

Jerusalem, January 8, 2001   The people of Israel didn't let Jerusalem down tonight. They turned out in the hundreds of thousands to pledge their allegiance to the Holy City as the undivided capital of Israel.

In a hastily planned event initiated by Yisrael B'Aliya leader Natan Sharansky, Jews from all over Israel and many countries in the Diaspora poured into the area just outside the walls of the Old City tonight to demonstrate their opposition to any move to redivide Jerusalem.

The Barak administration did its utmost to sabotage the event by sending out word through various emissaries that the rally was political, anti-government, and thus should not be supported by Jewish communities abroad. Today, the police issued dire statements warning of severe retribution against troublemakers at the rally — another attempt to keep people away by implying violence would erupt. In fact, the crowd is extraordinarily subdued and there's not a political sign to be seen. There are no pro-Sharon signs, nor anti-Barak placards. The banners are all focused on protecting Jerusalem.

"Jerusalem is Not Belfast, Berlin or Beirut," "The Temple Mount is Ours," read a few of the slogans displayed on huge banners hanging on the sides of the road right in front of Jaffa Gate and on up to Kikar Safra. The walls of the city are lit up, and every few yards there are people standing with their backs to the towering stones holding an Israeli flag, as if to protect the ancient structure with their bodies. At the appointed hour, the MC asks everyone to move away from the walls and into the streets, and the crowds swell as hundreds of buses disgorge their passengers from all over the country. The entire area, from Zion Gate past Jaffa Gate to New

Gate, down Jaffa Road to Kikar Zion, and all the way to King George Street, is jammed with people.

It's impossible to accurately estimate the crowd, but the MC announces that 400,000 are present, although the media count "only" 300,000. Unlike at the usual mass demonstrations in Tel Aviv's Kikar Rabin, there are no helicopters or traffic planes flying overhead to gauge the size of the assembly, but there's no question that this is a huge turnout.

There are more black hats in evidence than at regular demonstrations, and the crowd is overwhelmingly religious — but that just reflects the make up of Jerusalem. You can sense the resolve in people's faces, and the seriousness of the situation is reflected in the somber mood of those gathered.

While people continue to pour into the area, the Pirchei Yerushalayim Boy's Choir entertains with songs celebrating Jerusalem, ending with the anthem "Shalom al Yisrael." Huge torches are lit atop the gates of the city, and the almost full moon casts its silvery light over those assembled in the cool evening. The proceedings are projected onto the walls of the city itself, as subtle colored lighting illuminates the beautiful setting.

With the exception of Mayor Ehud Olmert, there are no political speakers. Former Supreme Court chief justice Moshe Landau; Rabbi Eli Sadan, head of the pre-army training program at Eli; Avital Sharansky, and Ronald Lauder, chair of the Conference of Presidents of Major American Jewish Organizations, are the main speakers. Israelis from all walks of life give short presentations explaining their attachment to the city — the English-speaking community is represented by author Naomi Ragen and Hindy Walfish, a more recent immigrant from New Jersey active in AMIT Women. Each presenter ends with the words: "Im eshkachaych Yerushalayim..." (If I forget You, O Jerusalem...)

Olmert makes a point of addressing US President Bill Clinton in Hebrew and English. After voicing his appreciation for Clinton's eight years of friendship to Israel and the Jewish people (a statement that is roundly booed by those standing around me) Olmert declares that it would be a shame if Clinton would now go down in history as the only US president who tried to divide Jerusalem.

Throughout the evening short film clips of the modern battles for Jerusalem are played. It's awesome to see the footage of the Israeli liberation of the Old City played on the very walls on which the historic event took place.

Tehillim (Psalms) are read, followed by 400,000 people singing "Im eshkachaych Yerushalayim..." and the recitation in unison of those ancient words.

A final prayer for the Israeli soldiers missing in action, those kidnapped, and imprisoned Israeli spy, Jonathan Pollard.

We watch one another's breath mingle in the cold night air as we stand at attention to sing Hatikva, and it seems as if we're invincible — surely Jerusalem could never fall again with so many of us united to protect her.

Those Holy Walls

Jerusalem, January 17, 2001   Esther Shlisser is crying as she approaches the imposing Hulda Gates on the southern side of the Temple Mount. The tears express the frustration, fear and disappointment of the 66-year-old native Jerusalem tour guide, as she leads a group of English speakers through the southern wall excavations.

Shlisser's blunt manner and encyclopedic knowledge are renowned among Jerusalem repeat tourists and residents who flock to her side to learn more about the Holy City.

But these days, Esther, a brunette with birdlike brown eyes and raspy voice, is exasperated with her government and her people. At the western corner of the southern wall, she yells for us to watch out for the dog and pigeon feces dotting the ancient steps. "Oy lanu (woe to us) that we allow this," she exclaims. "This place has the same kedusha (holiness) as the Western Wall, it was built at the same time. Those who believe that the Western Wall is our only holy site are liars. Where is Am Yisrael (the People of Israel)? Come here, let's clean the place. If WE don't think it's holy, what do you expect from our government," she continues.

Shlisser points to a huge pile of ancient stones on the western side of the Mount and indicates the hole they were dug from. She explains that holiness is not in the stones but in the place, the site. Once stones are removed from their holy place they lose their meaning.

We're the only group present in the entire area until a family with another English-speaking guide shows up. This too is upsetting to Shlisser. She tells us she comes every afternoon to pray mincha (the afternoon service) at the Hulda Gates on the southern wall. Under the Clinton proposal for Jerusalem, Israel would lose control over the southern wall, retaining sovereignty only over the

Western Wall and Jewish Quarter. "I don't call it the Jewish Quarter," Shlisser declares. "You can see a Jewish Quarter in Venice, a Moslem Quarter in Amman. Jerusalem IS Jewish...." "And by the way, you don't have to go to Poland to see destroyed synagogues — just look at the Old City under the Jordanians."

Before we move on to the majestic plaza of the Southern Wall, Shlisser directs our attention to a newly discovered mikveh (ritual bath) a few yards in front of the wall. Archaeologists have determined it's from the Second Temple period, and there are hundreds of mikvehs in the area. This was where the pilgrims arriving to pray at the Temple would ritually purify themselves before ascending to the holy site. The discovery is just another proof of Jewish claims to the Temple Mount. "What, did Moslems ever use a mikveh?" Shlisser snorts.

"At the base of the wall we see the remains of the stands where the Temple offerings were sold." "This is not Universal Studios," she says. We're walking in the footsteps of Hillel and Shammai.

Shlisser reminds us that there are 11 parshiot (Torah portions) which speak of the Beit Hamikdash, and 248 mitzvoth (commandments) which relate to the Temple. "And today we don't do enough for the Beit Hamikdash — what are YOU doing?" she asks us pointedly.

As we walk further along the southern wall, the sweet song of a lone bird breaks the heavy silence while we contemplate Esther's words.

She stops to point out the windows of the Al Aksa Mosque which dot the upper part of the southern wall. Above them, two new layers of stone have been added by Arabs over the past two months. Shlisser is outraged at the violation of the holiest Jewish site in the world. "I called the police about it. They told me they know all about it and it's being done with their permission," she relates incredulously. "We are so stupid. Even the Crusaders didn't dare build at Har Habayit," she spits out.

Before us we see the imposing Hulda Gates. In the first Temple period the area was called the Ophel — from the root "to ascend," because large numbers of Jews arrived to worship from the City of David to the south, just below. During Second Temple times there were two sets of Hulda Gates which are still visible today, even though they're completely blocked by huge stones — one triple arched gate, and one with double arches. Only a portion of the double arch is visible today, having been blocked off by the wall built by Suleiman the Great dissecting the Temple walls. Atop the wall sits barbed wire and a small security booth manned by an official from the Wakf — the Moslem Religious Authority which maintains de facto control over the entire Temple Mount area.

The Mishnah (Middot 2:2) describes these gates and the way in which people ascended to and descended from the Temple. The steps are of uneven size, so that running away from the Temple would have been impossible. Today, even though many of the steps leading up to the gates have been reconstructed, the tunnels used for access by the Cohanim (priests) are clearly visible.

We stand for a few moments at the top of the steps, before the imposing gates which lead to the Temple Mount. With my eyes tightly closed, I feel as if I am transported back thousands of years and my body could melt through the stone and emerge on the other side in the radiance of the Temple. Esther sheds her tears and we move on.

Protection, Israel style

Kfar Etzion, January 31, 2001   Even though he represents a district in the heart of Brooklyn, New York State Assemblyman Dov Hikind (D-Brooklyn) isn't used to dealing with bulletproof vests.

Yet today, Hikind spent the morning distributing some of the 90 Special Forces vests he has purchased with money donated by New York area politicians and constituents, and learning about the superior nature of Israeli-made protective equipment.

Governor George Pataki, Attorney-General Eliot Spitzer, Assembly Speaker Sheldon Silver, State Comptroller Carl McCall, Congressman Edolphus Towns, Bronx Borough President Fernando Ferrer and Brooklyn Borough President Howard Golden all contributed to the effort which raised $120,000 to pay for Israeli-made vests and helmets which will help protect the lives of medics and teachers traveling to their work in Judea, Samaria and Gaza.

A convoy of journalists, accompanied by Hikind and his aide Charni Sochet, made the journey to Kfar Etzion, the kibbutz whose entire adult population was massacred in 1948. After the Six Day War, when the area was recaptured by Israel, the children of the original settlers returned and re-established the kibbutz.

Today, one of Kfar Etzion's main industries is Mofet Etzion, one of the world's leading suppliers of ballistic armament protection. The money from New York is being used to buy the most sophisticated, highest level of protection vests manufactured anywhere in the world.

❖   ❖   ❖

Assemblyman Hikind brought with him a few vests he had purchased in New York. As he shleps them out of the box, the ambulance drivers who had arrived from Jewish communities all over the Gush look on with concern in their eyes. The hulking blue vests are heavy and cumbersome. They're fitted with ceramic pads and make movement difficult.

The cameras roll as Hikind attempts to don a vest. Shaking his head, Hikind still can't quite grasp what he's doing. "I would never have believed that I'd be coming to Israel to give out bulletproof jackets just so people could get to work," he exclaims. In New York, no government authority would tolerate citizens being shot or stoned as they travel the highways of the state, Hikind notes.

But the U.S.-made vests are only to illustrate Hikind's point. The bulk of the equipment which will go to the YESHA medics and teachers will be from Mofet Etzion. Gush Etzion Regional Council head Shaul Goldstein and Security Coordinator Benny Kadosh step forward to open the Israeli-made vests and present the first one for Hikind to give over to the assembled medics.

As the light-weight black jackets emerge from their boxes, Hikind is visibly moved and astonished when the white logo on the vest emerges. 'One Israel Fund/YESHA, Dov Hikind' in English letters is inscribed over the heart. Goldstein tells Hikind that anyone who pays as much attention to the residents of YESHA as Hikind does deserves the recognition and, in fact, "your caring makes it as if you're living here," he says.

The medics and Kfar Etzion residents who are on hand to watch the brief ceremony smile and nod their assent. Goldstein, a clean-shaven man in his thirties, remarks to Hikind that if Rina Didovsky and Sara Leisha had been wearing the Hikind vests, they would be alive today. The two teachers were murdered in separate terrorist incidents over the past two months.

The ambulance drivers come over to thank Hikind, load the vests into their vehicles and drive off. Hikind is invited to meet the directors of Mofet Etzion, and we follow through the tranquil grounds of the kibbutz to a brand new building not far from the dining room. David Ramati, senior product engineer, explains the workings of this extraordinary company. David, born in the United States, has lived in Israel for decades. He's held various security positions with the IDF, as well as in hotspots throughout YESHA.

Mofet Etzion has built its reputation on the invention of Dr. Michael Cohen, a brilliant Israeli ballistics engineer who developed the Light Improved Ballistic Armor (LIBA) concept. LIBA has revolutionized the defense industry all over the world. Cohen, a large jovial man with a teddy-bear like appearance, explains through a translator that, until the latest violence, most of the company's business was abroad. Mofet Etzion supplies its material to the US Marine Corps, the Dutch army and the Canadian Armed Forces.

The revolutionary concept provides extremely light-weight but super-strong material that can withstand almost every kind of assault. LIBA is used to protect tanks, armored cars, and now school buses and people in Israel.

Hikind is clearly thrilled that the money he's brought from New York will be spent here in Israel, but it's still difficult for the longtime politician to fully grasp the ballistic concepts we're seeing in the offices of Mofet Etzion. For a more graphic demonstration we're taken to the testing tunnel, where Hikind is handed a set of heavy-duty earplugs. The room is completely padded with gray egg-carton like foam. Ramati and Dr. Cohen show us the bullets which are about to be fired at different ranges into one of their vests — one from a Kalashnikov and another from a smaller pistol. Ramati points out that the PA police have a preference for armor-piercing tracer bullets.

After the bullets are fired, Ramati rips open the LIBA fortified vest. The thin yellow, plastic-like material is not even marked. In a traditional bulletproof vest some of the layers are pierced after one shooting, rendering the vest unusable. What is even more amazing to Hikind and the press gathered around is that the two-inch bullets we saw a moment before have been reduced to tiny harmless button-size disks of metal. Hikind is given a few to take home as souvenirs.

Back outside in the bright sunshine, Hikind finally appreciates what he and his New York friends have purchased for some of the people of YESHA — a little more security and peace of mind.

Election Madness

Jerusalem, January 30, 2001   Democracy works differently here in the Middle East. Maybe it's because there isn't any other democratic country in this part of the world that Israeli elections have become so quirky.

Here in Israel, every night for the three weeks before the elections, anyone who happens to be home trying to enjoy an evening of TV entertainment is subjected to ten minutes of party campaign broadcasts on both Israeli channels. The campaign blurbs run back to back, alternating between Ariel Sharon and Ehud Barak, and, unlike in America or England, where repetition is the name of the game, here, the enterprising copywriters come up with new material every night. People actually discuss the jingles and the message at the water cooler the next day.

Tonight Barak's theme is the dove of peace. The former prime minister (easy to forget that he resigned weeks ago) waxes poetic about how fervently he wants peace, while images of war flash across the screen. The closing slogan is "The Choice is Peace."

Sharon invokes the legacy of Menahem Begin. We see newspaper headlines from the Begin election campaign proclaiming that Begin will not bring peace — precisely the same accusation leveled against Sharon today. Then images of Begin with Carter and Sadat flash across the screen. The closing slogan is "Sharon, A Leader for Peace."

All the blurbs have Russian subtitles to cater to the 19 percent of the electorate who are immigrants from the FSU. According to most polls, the "Russian" vote is overwhelmingly in Sharon's camp. Barak's people try to say that's because the immigrants know nothing of Sharon's history in Lebanon, but most Jews from the FSU I talk to are as disappointed with Barak as the rest of Israel and just see Sharon as a stronger leader.

"The immigrants feel something they felt in the past — that the ground is shaking under their feet," says Dov Kontorer, a columnist at Vesti, Israel's largest Russian-language daily.

"They saw a large empire disintegrate before their eyes. Now they are afraid that something like that can happen in this small, vulnerable country. They feel threatened and in danger," Kontorer adds, explaining the reason a majority of immigrants favor Sharon.

Even those who can't yet vote are pulled into election fever. Kids are an integral element of election campaigns here. It's impossible to halt at the traffic light of any intersection in the country without having bumper stickers and election material thrust through your car window by aggressive teenagers. They're the ones who every night hang the banners along the highways and over every available fence in the cities — and they're the ones who tear down the opposition's materials every night, too.

High school mock elections here are serious events covered by the media. Blich High School in Ramat Gan has traditionally predicted the winner in almost every election over the past 30 years — this year they picked Ehud Barak. The candidates stop off at numerous high schools all over the country during the campaign. One teenager made international headlines last week when she confronted Sharon at her school in Beersheva. Today, the 16-year-old daughter of Aryeh Hershkowitz, killed in a terrorist attack the day before, was asked in a radio broadcast what she would say to Ehud Barak.

Some groups vote en masse, following the candidate their leader tells them to vote for. So far, Shas, the party made up largely of Sephardic Jews with religious leanings, is backing Sharon, and a recent court ruling may widen their campaigning. Shas leaders like to distribute blessings with voting suggestions attached, but the distribution of amulets or gifts is strictly forbidden under election law. In order to comply with the law, the party was ordered to print its blessings on paper rather than parchment and attach a letter from party leader Eli Yishai saying that the blessing is not a good luck charm.

It will take more than blessings and charms to get out the vote in the Arab sector. Israeli Arabs make up 12 percent of the voting public. According to Hebrew University Arab affairs expert Dr. Yitzhak Reiter, more than 75 percent of the Arab voters participated in the last election, with 97 percent of them voting for Ehud Barak. Today, a coalition of Arab parties and movements issued a call to their voters to boycott the upcoming elections, to protest the killing of Israeli Arabs who rioted against Israeli police last October. At a mass demonstration in Nazareth yesterday, protestors waved Palestinian flags and held placards with the pictures of the 13 victims.

The so called "petek lavan" (white/blank note) option is an idea also bandied about by many Israeli Jews as a way to register their protest at not having a candidate who represents their choice. In essence, in this election, the blank vote becomes a vote for Sharon, since the majority of those who say they will cast the blank ballot are the self-defined left.

But all who do place the yellow slip with the name of their candidate of choice into the envelope and slip it into the slot of the traditional ballot box know that their votes will be counted. No worries about chads and dimples here in the only democracy in the Middle East.

Decision Day

Jerusalem, Election Day, 2001   The people of Israel have spoken with as close to one voice as they ever have. Despite the lowest turnout in any election since the founding of the state, a massive landslide of those who did vote cast their ballots for a new prime minister and rejected outright the policies and negotiating style of Ehud Barak.

Now that Barak has resigned and bowed out of the political arena, and Arik Sharon has made his victory speech, we can sit and look back over election day here.

Already this morning the turnout looked sparse. A little after 8 a.m. a dejected friend called to say there was no one at the polling place in the secular neighborhood where she went to vote.

Several hours later, urgent e-mail messages wound their way to various right-wing newslists describing the low turnout and urging people to come out and vote.

At my Jerusalem polling station, a high school next door to the residence of Mayor Ehud Olmert, there was a slow but steady flow of concerned voters. The ground leading to the polling place was strewn with official yellow voting slips by the time I showed up to exercise my civic duty at around 11 a.m. Despite Israel's high tech society, voting here is still conducted the old fashioned way — by placing a yellow slip printed with the name of the candidate of choice in an envelope, and then dropping it into a blue cardboard ballot box. This election we were presented with three piles of slips in the booth: Ariel Sharon, Ehud Barak and blank ballots. One enterprising last minute campaigner had pocketed a large quantity of Sharon voting slips and tucked one under the windshield wiper of every car in the neighborhood.

According to police reports, some 185 incidents requiring police intervention took place at or near polling stations across the country. Outside every one of the 7,400 polling places at least one IDF soldier was stationed. Security guards were much in evidence inside the buildings, too, and party monitors sat in every classroom where ballots were cast, to make sure there were no irregularities.

The mood in the line snaking into the classrooms was quiet and somber. No one seemed too happy with the choices placed before us, but most voters who bothered to show up acknowledged the need for a change.

Back on the streets, Israelis enjoyed a rare day off without religious responsibilities. The weather cooperated and it felt like a Friday. The cafes were full, but one topic of conversation dominated the din. When I sat down at a favorite streetside spot on Emek Refayim, the traffic proved more interesting than the conversation. A carload of yeshiva students barreled down the street, with black-hatted young men leaning out of back and front windows waving Sharon banners. Two minutes later, two white sedans completely covered with Barak paraphernalia came honking down the street.

At the school up the street, where voters were filing in, an enterprising junior high school kid had set up shop at the entrance with coffee and cookies to ease the pain of those who felt compelled to hold their noses as they voted for the lesser of two evils.

As one of the sixty percent of voters who chose Arik over Ehud, I happily accepted an invitation to a victory party after the polls closed. Walking up the street near the Jerusalem Theater, I heard the loud blasts of a shofar and the pop of champagne corks over the rooftops from the balcony of my friend's apartment. Many of the people in the room had taken an active role in the Sharon campaign, and emotions were high as we gathered round the television to hear the exit poll results and listen to the speeches. It was fascinating to watch the foreign media at Sharon HQ. They were so clearly put out by the results. One could see it in their body language and hear it in their interviews of various Likud figures.

At several points during Sharon's remarks, the members of the Young Likud, a largely secular band of young politicos, started chanting "Har Habayit B'yadeynu." (The Temple Mount is in our hands.) It's clear that Barak completely misread the Israeli public, who just couldn't abide his willingness to concede parts of Jerusalem to Arafat.

One can only imagine what the results would have been had Netanyahu run against Barak — certainly many people who just couldn't bring themselves to vote Sharon would have gone over to Bibi. He was nowhere to be seen on the long platform when Sharon gave his inaugural speech as prime-minister-elect. Sadly, there'll be no first lady — Lilly Sharon passed away last year. So Sharon relies on his son Omri for familial support.

Now we brace for an escalation of Arab violence (14 documented shooting attacks took place throughout YESHA today), but trust that, with the strong mandate of the people, our new leader will have the strength to formulate a realistic policy which will prioritize the security needs of our people.

Shalhevet's Funeral

Hebron, April 1, 2001   Have you ever been to the funeral of a 10-month-old? It has to be one of the most unnatural of human experiences.

Maybe you've attended the funeral of a baby who died tragically from Sudden Infant Death Syndrome or some other dreadful disease — but the burial of an infant who was deliberately murdered by terrorists is all the more tragic for the baseless hate it represents.

Today, in the ancient cemetery of Hebron, Shalhevet Techiya Pass was laid to rest next to Torah luminaries such as the Sde Hemed and Reishit Hochma, and beside other Jews who were victims of earlier Arab hatred. Perhaps there are tombstones of other young children in the hillside burial place of the 1929 Hebron massacre victims, but there are no younger terror targets than Shalhevet buried there.

Bullet-proof buses brought mourners from Jerusalem along the tunnel road into Gush Etzion, past Efrat, and through the deceptively peaceful rural Judean hills dotted with Arab villages, and on into Hebron. Men with black hats; knitted kippot; large, white Reb Nachman-style kippot and a few with T-shirts tied around their heads crowded onto the buses, making room for young women holding babies of Shalhevet's age. A few women wearing pants joined the subdued crowd.

Along the way, groups of sullen Arab men could be seen hanging around otherwise deserted storefronts, as well as IDF soldiers checking cars and taxis trying to leave Arab villages under closure.

Several thousand gathered in front of the imposing Maarat Hamachpelah (Cave of the Patriarchs) — the most ancient Jewish site in the world. The structure was built during the Second Temple period and stands on the field that Abraham purchased some 3700 years ago.

In the forecourt, under the hot midday sun, sit Shalhevet's grieving family. Parents, grandparents, uncles and aunts, they brace themselves for the difficult hours to come. Almost a week has passed since the murder of their baby, but with the advice of their rabbi, they had postponed the burial demanding that the IDF retake the Abu Sneinah hills which harbored the terrorist who took Shalhevet's life. The burial today is an acknowledgment that at least the issue has received prominent national attention, and it will allow the Pass family to complete the full shiva period before the commencement of Passover.

The media feeding frenzy is in full operation as the proceedings begin. Cameramen crowd around Shalhevet's father, Yitzhak Pass, who is pushed in a wheelchair to the stage where the microphone will broadcast the words of eulogy and Psalms to the crowd. The young man, whose bright, smiling countenance graced the pages of every Israeli newspaper last week as he held his contented child, is now ashen-faced. Released from the hospital just before Shabbat, the shot wounds to his legs sustained as he tried to protect Shalhevet still prevent him from walking. Yitzhak wears a yellow baseball style cap emblazoned with the slogan: We are Here.

As the Psalms begin, many mourners are quietly sobbing. Yitzhak clutches tissues in his hand and grabs the arm of his father-in-law for support. Rabbi Dov Lior of Kiryat Arba, gives the first eulogy, a fiery speech calling for the government to avenge the murder of Shalhevet. In a wavering, child-like voice, the baby's teenage aunt recalls Shalhevet's sweet smile. Before moving off to accompany the body to the cemetery, another relative cries out the powerful "Hashem, Hashem, Keyl Rahum V'Chanun" prayer. The verses from Exodus are from the time when Moses went to receive the second set of Tablets. God shows Moses how to prevent the type of national catastrophe that had nearly provoked Him to wipe out the nation. Moses is taught the text of the prayer that would always invoke God's mercy, and which is generally recited on Yom Kippur and in times of crisis. Our current situation, where innocent babies

"Shalhevet Pass, your blood cries out: Put the IDF Back in Abu Sneinah!"
Sign in front of Abu Sneinah hills, Hebron.

and high school children are murdered in the Jewish state, clearly qualifies.

The tiny body, draped in a dark blue velvet cover adorned with a gold Star of David, is carried through the streets of Hebron where Shalhevet spent the brief days of her life. In separate columns, men and women follow, chanting the Sephardic tune to Eishet Chayil (A Woman of Worth). Many of the mourners wear pictures of Shalhevet around their necks.

All the stores are shuttered and the streets empty of their Arab residents — a strict curfew has been imposed to ensure safety. Dozens of IDF soldiers line the route and are three deep at Gross Square in front of the closed road leading to Abu Sneinah.

A short stop at the Avraham Avinu neighborhood where Shalhevet was murdered, and then on up King David Street under the watchful eyes of the IDF and border police, past the Jewish residential buildings of Beit Hadassah, Beit Romano and Beit Schneerson.

In the crowd of quiet marchers the only public figures visible are former MKs Geula Cohen and Elyakim Haetzni, MK Yuri Shtern and former Prisoner of Zion Yosef Mendelevich. No cabinet ministers or representatives of the Sharon government are present.

Several high profile media people are there however, most noticeably the portly Jerrold Kessel of CNN, with a misshapen black and white hat pulled down over his eyes.

The procession wends its way under the harsh sun, up the short, steep hill of Tarpat Street and into the cemetery gates. At some point, Yitzhak Pass, immobilized in his wheelchair, holds the body of Shalhevet on his knees. At her graveside, there are more eulogies given by Hebron pioneer, Rabbi Moshe Levinger, and by Rabbi Yosef Mendelevich, the modest hero whose actions in Leningrad in 1970 forced open the gates of freedom for millions of Jews from the FSU.

As teenagers hug each other to try to contain their grief, and men close their eyes deep in prayer, the mournful prayer for mercy is sobbed out again before Yitzhak barely manages to intone the mourner's kaddish for his only child.

Another brutal act of hatred enters the annals of Jewish consciousness, as the unnatural act of burying a murdered baby is completed.

Journalists Behaving Badly

Florence, May 2, 2001   Ofer Bavly, from the Israeli Embassy in Rome, and Ali Rashid, PLO representative in Rome, sat next to each other exchanging friendly banter.

Things weren't so cordial up on stage where two Israeli journalists, a Palestinian human rights worker and a Jewish New York magazine editor sparred over the state of press freedom in Israel and the Palestine Authority.

The debate took place in Florence at a conference celebrating International Press Freedom Day organized by Informazione senze Frontiere (ISF) (Information Without Borders) an Italian non-profit group.

To the surprise of the Europeans, the tension was most pronounced between the two Israelis, Haaretz reporter Gideon Levy and me. Levy, best known for his weekly columns describing the misery of Palestinians living in the territories, took great exception to my description of Palestine Authority corruption and autocracy, accusing me of "patronizing and preaching" to Palestinians and being blind to Israeli shortcomings. Levy maintains that Israel is not a democratic state since it "occupies another people."

Levy's take on IDF actions: "All those guys perpetrating so many cruel actions toward a people who fights for its independence." A slight smile crept over the face of fellow panelist, Bassam Eid, director of the Palestine Human Rights Monitoring Group, as Levy spoke. Eid's remarks to the small audience gathered in the imposing Florentine hall consisted of an attack on the bias of the media in Israel, and nostalgic recollections of cooperative relations between Palestinians and Israeli journalists during the first intifada.

The three of us had traveled from Tel Aviv together and arrived in

Florence after a bizarre journey that involved spending the night parked alongside the autostrada when our bus broke down. That should have been a bonding experience, but I could tell that the two friends were wondering why I had been invited to take part in the conference. In fact, all of us had been suggested by a mutual acquaintance, Riccardo Cristiano, the disgraced Italian journalist who was stripped of his Israeli press credentials after a letter he wrote appeared in a Ramallah daily.

Eid and Levy knew Cristiano from his four-year stint as Jerusalem correspondent for the Italian Government TV channel. As for me, I had interviewed Cristiano in Rome last December for an article on Palestinian intimidation of foreign journalists, and we'd kept in touch.

Since his unauthorized letter, apologizing for the actions of a rival independent TV station that passed footage of the Ramallah lynchings on to the Israeli Embassy in Rome, Cristiano has been demoted. He now covers the pope for the government radio station. So, he stayed around while we discussed the conference agenda with members of the ISF, but was conspicuously absent from the conference itself where representatives of the Italian Union of Journalists and the Italian deputy minister of information were in attendance. He told us he was off to Athens to cover the pope's visit there, two days early.

Those in the audience were largely European journalists, together with officials of the various unions and federations that proliferate in countries with socialist tendencies. Did any of them realize that Cristiano had arranged a most unrepresentative group of guests? Levy, an Israeli chronicler of Palestinian suffering; Eid, a Palestinian critical of the PA, and myself, an American immigrant writing in English for papers outside Israel.

Most participants seemed likewise unaware of the well-documented repressive attitude of the PA toward their fellow journalists. When I raised this issue, using concrete examples from interviews with foreign reporters in Jerusalem, I was met with stony silence. In contrast, Bassam Eid's strange, out of context closing remarks received wide applause.

Eid, who was sweating profusely as he recounted the tale, spoke of the MSNBC poll to determine the picture of the year. One of the pictures was of Muhammad Al Dura, the 12-year-old who was killed at Netzarim junction in the early days of the anti-Jewish violence. Eid avers that the Israeli consul general in Los Angeles started a campaign e-mailing and calling everyone he knew to vote against that picture. "I was at Tom Segev's house," Eid noted, relishing mention of the post-Zionist author's name. "We voted, and Segev then put out a letter critical of the LA consul."

Eid and Levy were taken by our hosts for appearances on local TV and radio shows. I was not invited. No doubt Levy repeated comments he made at the conference: "It's not for me to be proud of the Israeli press...." Accusing the Israeli media of self-censorship in writing about the Palestinians, Levy told his European counterparts at the conference, "Most Israelis are concentrated solely on themselves, never seeing the other. Whether it's foreign workers, new immigrants or Palestinians, they don't see them as human beings." With the approving glance of his friend Bassam, Levy went on to ask rhetorically whether there were only Jewish and Israeli victims of the conflict. "That's the impression you get from our media," he asserted.

After this session there was no eye contact between us, and little conversation, despite the fact that we were staying at the same hotel and traveling back to Israel together.

Levy did break the silence to tell me the most abusive e-mail he receives is from American Jews.

Day of the Knitted Kipot

Jerusalem, May 21, 2001 Last year we celebrated Jerusalem Day under the threat of the Barak/Clinton plan that would have hacked off chunks of the eastern flank of the city and given them over to Arafat control. One can only shudder to think of the devastating effects had such a move been actualized.

Today, the day commemorating the 34th anniversary of the reunification of Jerusalem was observed by a shrinking portion of the population.

Whether because of security fears, apathy, or the general malaise that has Israelis increasingly in its grip, Yom Yerushalayim was celebrated mainly by the national religious community.

This was apparent at events all over the city: at the "To Jerusalem With Love" concert last night at Hechal Shlomo; the walking tours all over the city; this morning's march of the Temple Faithful through eastern Jerusalem; the crowd viewing the exhibits and trenches at Ammunition Hill; the parade of flags later in the day that brought thousands of youth to the capital; the festive evening concert at the Kotel — all had one thing in common. Clearly a majority of those taking part were observant. This was the day of the knitted kipa.

It seems that secular Israelis have tired of expressions of nationalism. But for the tens of thousands who did turn out to celebrate, it was a welcome opportunity to publicly reaffirm their commitment to the capital of the Jewish people, as well as to let loose a little.

A poll released today showed nearly seven out of ten Israelis "very worried" by the country's security plight, and more than six out of ten convinced that a new Middle East war is near.

Today's events went off with no serious security problems. The thousands of youngsters who stayed up most of the night singing

---

and dancing at Yeshivat Beit Orot walked down to the Kotel in the early morning without incident.

Gershom Solomon's small band of Temple Faithful marched down Route #1 to the PA's Jerusalem headquarters, Orient House, where they met vociferous, but peaceful Palestinian opposition.

Tens of thousands white-shirted, flag-bearing teenagers flooded the closed off streets of central Jerusalem, singing and dancing as they made their way to the Kotel. Hundreds of police, border patrol and IDF kept a close watch on their progress.

Arab stores in the Old City market were tightly shuttered as waves of people flooded down the ancient alleys toward the Wall. Passing quickly through the security barriers, they joined the huge party that filled almost every corner of the Kotel plaza.

From my vantage point on the balcony of an apartment overlooking the plaza, the view was awe-inspiring. The mechitza separating men from women had been extended to the back of the plaza, and behind it, thousands of teens formed a mass of joyful exuberance. Waving Israeli flags, some jumped up and down to the lively music, while others formed graceful, vibrant circles of dancers.

The voice of Natan Sharansky rang out over the throng as he urged Jews to unite to protect Jerusalem.

Tonight, the amplified voice of prayer broadcasting from the Temple Mount was ours, not that of the muezzin heard five times a day. The huge, orderly crowd was our kids celebrating a seminal event in modern Jewish history, not hundreds of cousins who stream out of the Al Aksa mosque every Friday to hurl stones at Jews below.

In the Jewish Quarter the cafes were brimming with customers. The main square was packed with people enjoying a respite from the tension-filled moments of the past months.

Too bad secular Israel wasn't there to share in the moment.

Holding Up Under Fire

May, 2001   "I feel I'm beginning to look my age," says Cheryl Mandel, long time resident of Alon Shvut in Gush Etzion, south of Jerusalem, "because of the tension caused by the past months of Arab violence."

Mandel remarks that, when she made aliya 14 years ago, she was struck by how much younger she looked than her Israeli peers. The years of tension and stress had taken their toll on the Israeli women. Now, Mandel feels she has joined their ranks.

The continuing attacks against Jews have caused significant lifestyle changes for many Israelis, but mothers living in YESHA are among the most affected.

Mandel feels the tension in her muscles as she waits for her 12th grade son to return from basketball practice in Jerusalem. As part of a semi-pro team, Gabriel has to be in the city five nights per week. By the time he's ready to come home, the last bulletproof bus has already left. So Gabriel stands at the entrance to the tunnel road waiting for a ride for the 15-minute journey home.

The road is often closed because of shooting attacks from Arab villages overlooking the area. Three Jewish residents of Gush Etzion have been killed on this road, and stoning and shooting attacks are now routine. Many people wear bulletproof jackets and helmets while driving to and from Jerusalem these days.

So Cheryl lies awake until Gabriel walks in the door. By now, she's already been in touch with her son by cell-phone several times since he set out for home. The most important call is to let her know that someone's stopped to pick him up and they're on the road. Then she knows exactly how long the journey home should take.

Some parents of younger children have made a conscious decision not to take their children on the roads unless absolutely necessary. Eve Harow is an Efrat mother of seven children ranging in age from 4-18. Rather than take the kids to the mall at the other end of the tunnel road, Harow buys clothes and shoes for her younger kids and brings them home for them to try on.

Lately, the Harow family hasn't been able to observe its birthday tradition either. Until last year, one part of every child's birthday celebration was a family dinner at the kosher Burger King in Jerusalem. Now they stay home rather than submit to what Harow describes as "the feeling of vulnerability" on the roads.

But like Cheryl Mandel's boys, several of the Harow children are involved in extra-curricular activities that take them outside the Gush. Two of her teenagers play on Little League teams. "None of the other teams will come to Efrat now," Harow explains. "So our team has to be on the roads more to get to games."

Another Efrat resident, Shana Mauer, notes that evenings out are a rarity, because of the frequent road closures, the danger of being on the roads at night, and because many people prefer not to be in the same vehicle as their spouse.

Some communities have organized additional activities for the children and teens, and some parents in Gush Katif communities have signed up for cable TV in order to keep their kids inside, preferring to expose them to questionable culture rather than to mortar shells.

The added stress of living under the threat of violence has caused physical effects too. Mandel refers to people she knows whose eating habits have deteriorated. "We sometimes find ourselves sitting in front of the TV news with candy in our hands," she says. Others have taken up smoking to try to handle the strain. Mandel's married daughter, a drama teacher, vomited from anxiety after a difficult trip home from Jerusalem kept her from her two small children hours longer than anticipated.

To date, Gush Katif has been the most embattled area in the violent Arab assault. Jewish villages there have sustained the most consistent bombardment from their hostile neighbors in Khan Yunis. Israelis have been living for months now with the knowledge

179

that they will be attacked every night. Everyone deals with the situation in his or her own way.

Roberta Bienenfeld, who has lived in Neve Dekalim, Gush Katif, for over 20 years had this to say:

> We are living under constant bombardment. This means that we hear shooting, bombing and mortars both day and night. Not a day passes that we don't hear shooting. Sometimes it is real, at other times it is a door slamming, the wind blowing in the trees, boys bouncing a basketball on the nearby basketball court. You could call it being shell-shocked.
>
> And although there are sometimes incidents during the day, we know that at night there WILL be shooting. The question is when. Your ears are always cocked, waiting, just waiting for something to happen. Once you hear it, you can begin to relax. Usually it occurs between 10 p.m. and midnight. You try to get your kids to sleep before then.

Bienenfeld says that, for her, the shooting has become such a day-to-day occurrence that she doesn't even really hear it anymore. "One of the jokes around here is that if there isn't any shooting, you can't fall asleep."

"The truth is that I, at least, don't feel that I am living under terror, which of course I am. I am very aware of every little noise, helicopters overhead, constant news on the television and radio. But G-d has given us ways of ignoring it and has allowed us to get used to a new reality. Shooting becomes the norm. Announcements to stay inside the same."

Bienenfeld, who made aliya from New York, explains that each child experiences the effect of the war in a unique way. Her oldest child is finishing the second year of national service in the neighboring community of Netzarim. Her 11th grade daughter will be eligible to earn extra points on her Bagruyot (national high school tests) since she lives in an area affected by the violence, but Bienenfeld acknowledges that her grades have suffered this year. Her youngest daughter moved into her sister's room, so that she

Bullet-proof Egged bus on route 160 from Jerusalem to Gush Etzion and Hebron.

would be on the side of the house as far away from Khan Yunis as possible.

Seeing their children deal with funerals and shiva calls saddens many parents. "I'd never been to funerals at that age," Cheryl Mandel observes sadly. The absence of a carefree childhood and normal freedoms are painful results of the current situation. The constant checking in with parents and restricted movement and activities are difficult to deal with for parents and children.

On the positive side, the situation has in fact strengthened feelings of solidarity and resolve both within families and within the settlements. According to Shani Simkowitz of Tekoa, the horrible events experienced by Tekoa residents have made them come together as an extended family. "The quality of life here can't be bought," she says. "People care for one another, look out for each other and share in the tragedies," Simkowitz says of the small, heterogeneous community in the Judean hills. "This is our strength, this is what's getting us through," she says.

Many women in the most severely affected communities are deeply attuned to the spiritual aspect of the situation. For some, it has been difficult to explain to their children why tragedies are happening all around them. "It's a stretch for emunah (faith)," sighs Eve Harow. "Where was Hashem when those two 14-year-old boys from Tekoa were brutalized and murdered," she wonders out

181

loud. "We just don't know," she answers herself, noting that the same question has resonated through centuries of greater Jewish suffering before there was a state and an army to protect Jews.

Cheryl Mandel, observant herself, expresses jealousy of those whom she perceives to have deep faith. "They seem to be managing better. I envy them their clarity and strength," she says. In a moment of introspection, Mandel explains that, until this year, she would have described herself as positive, outgoing, optimistic and strong. "Now, I feel anxious, worried, not at all optimistic and despondent," she says, quickly adding that by nature she's not pessimistic, and is grateful to her psychologist husband who "keeps things in perspective."

Like many others, Mandel's work life has suffered from the intifada. She manages the Etzion Judaica Center not far from her home. Since October, not one tour bus has stopped at the unique Judaica gallery and store. Now, Mandel and her staff are adapting to the new reality by emphasizing items for the local market. "We'll get through this difficult period and keep the jewel of the Gush sparkling," she notes.

Underlying the anxiety, fear, sadness and despondency, there's a spirit of defiance and a sense of destiny that sustains those living through these hard times.

"We're going to grow and prosper," says Shani Simkowitz of Tekoa. "People have to realize that this is not a "settler" problem, it's a Jewish problem, and they better realize we have finally come home and we're choosing to stay."

Eve Harow, who moved to the new Efrat neighborhood of Zayit with 11 other families just before Passover, reminds herself and her children that a few brave Jews have been on the firing line in every generation. Now it's their turn, and she's proud to have the privilege of making Jewish history. "We're very determined to stay and to build. We're not going anywhere."

Girding for War

Jerusalem, June 6, 2001   Thirty-four years ago today, Jerusalem witnessed perhaps the most decisive battles of the Six Day War. On June 6, 1967, Israeli troops captured almost all of East Jerusalem outside the city walls in order to stop Arab attacks against Jewish vehicles from the neighborhoods of Abu Tor, Silwan, Sheik Jarrah and French Hill. The fierce battle of Ammunition Hill was fought on this date, thirty-four years ago.

Today, it felt as if the citizens of Jerusalem were girding for battle once more.

At a massive prayer vigil called by the country's leading rabbis, thousands of concerned Israelis jam the plaza in front of the Western Wall to cry out for God's mercy in these dreadful times. The crowd fills almost every corner of the holy site.

Led by prominent Sephardic and Ashkenazic rabbis, the throng stands for more than ninety minutes, reciting prayers from a four-page sheet passed through the crowd. Several of the prayers are taken from the Yom Kippur ritual, emphasizing the gravity of the occasion.

But the shofar blasts heard tonight are not so much calling us to an inner accounting-rather they proclaim the gathering of the tribe and its readiness to engage, with God's help, in another battle against those who would destroy us.

The latest tragedy, a 5-month-old baby who barely clings to life after a rock was hurled at his head as he traveled in a car last night with his young parents, makes clear the need to bring the present situation to an end.

On the road winding from Dung Gate to Sultan's Pools, soldiers are stationed every fifty yards or so. One group stops several young Arabs standing over a pile of rocks.

Many of those who gathered at the Wall make their way into

town after the conclusion of the prayer vigil to take part in the demonstration organized by the YESHA council and other right wing groups. The slogan on the banner framing the podium in Zion Square is "Let's Beat Arafat."

Organizers are careful to point out that this is not an anti-Sharon protest, but an anti-Arafat demonstration. Speakers include Moshe Arens, Effie Eitam and Yitzhak Levy. Eitam, a former high level army officer who resigned in protest over policies of the Barak administration, threatens that if Prime Minister Sharon will not change his policy of restraint, "we'll have to find someone else, who will do it."

There is no more talk of peace here. Arafat, Fatah and Hamas have made it abundantly clear to all but the most obtuse, wishful-thinking, far leftists, that their hatred of Jews knows no bounds. When infants, as well as teens at a disco, are targets, the writing is on the wall.

In 1967 Israeli leaders knew what they had to do. Today, the people are ready. Let's hope our leaders get the message.

Davka!

Jerusalem, June 10, 2001   Ever see a 10 year old with kippa and tzitzit (ritual fringes) dancing an Irish jig? If you had been in the courtyard of the Jerusalem Theater tonight, you would have witnessed that sight.

The scene took place at one of the free concerts that make up part of the annual five week Israel Festival here. A six piece Israeli band dedicated to Irish music regaled hundreds of Jerusalemites who showed up to enjoy an evening of free outdoor entertainment.

Featuring some of the world's best artists, like conductor Daniel Barenboim; diva Dame Kiri Te Kanawa and jazz great Max Roach, the festival has provided Israelis with the opportunity to demonstrate our resolve not to succumb to the efforts of Arab terrorists to make us close down the country out of fear.

Before tonight's concert, the plaza of the theater was turned over to children's entertainers. Magicians, fire-throwers, balloon artists and musicians all took up positions in separate corners of the spacious area. Kids wandered around munching on cotton candy and popcorn, while their parents enjoyed a beer or cappuccino purchased from stands on the periphery.

A dozen disabled kids and their counselors (all religious teens) took their places in the front row for the concert. Every seat in the place was filled before the bagpipes, accordion and drums started up.

A similar scene took place last Thursday night at another Festival event entitled: "Love is in the Air." The venue for this spectacle was the ancient Sultan's Pool amphitheater, just below the walls of the Old City and the Tower of David.

I arrived early with three friends, and we took our seats dejectedly among only a few hundred others present. We grumbled that people were scared to come out to big public events, but as we

185

looked toward the entrances, we began to see crowds streaming into the area. By the time the program started, almost all 5,000 seats were filled.

The savvy Jerusalemites could be distinguished from the visiting students, who showed up in T-shirts and shorts, still carrying with them the heat of the day. We huddled in our sweatshirts and jackets against the chill Jerusalem night air, but a great time was had by all.

The set was unusual and creative — a blaze of vivid color and light. The musical acts were terrific too. Well-known Israeli contemporary singers — most slightly older than those popular in the US or Great Britain — wowed the crowd with lively numbers. Eli Luzon, a powerful albino singer, sang a few numbers with a beautiful young Ethiopian Jewish vocalist named Ayala Ingedshet. Yehudit Ravitz and Barry Sacharoff had the young people in the audience dancing in the aisles and singing along with their songs. The energy was palpable, as everyone let off steam at the end of another difficult week marked by the funerals of 21 young disco goers. The MC, as well as Micha Lewensohn, Israel Festival director, made a point of thanking the people of Jerusalem for coming out to the concert.

Not to be outdone, the English-speaking community turned out in force for yet another cultural event — a semi-professional performance of the musical Guys and Dolls. The show had played to packed houses in Jerusalem, but I hadn't managed to get there. I went to the opening night of the production in Jaffa. The Noga Theater is about three blocks from the Dolphinarium disco. The show opened four days after the suicide bomb attack that claimed 21 young lives, but the theater was mobbed. Outdoor cafes next to the theater were filled with patrons, determined to enjoy their evening out.

The opening of the annual Hebrew Book Week fair was postponed for two days out of respect for the grieving families of the Dolphinarium tragedy. But when it did open last Monday, Safra Square in the center of Jerusalem was filled with bargain seekers and browsers. The week-long event brings publishers of every kind of book out to peddle their wares. From slick coffee table volumes to esoteric Talmudic commentaries; brightly colored children's books to the serious publications of all the major Israeli universities — it's a bibliophile's dream.

All these cultural events were conducted with the usual heavy security precautions, and all went off without a hitch. Life here goes on in the face of Arab threats of continued violence.

Arafat has badly misjudged the Israeli character if he thinks he'll bring the country to its knees by terror tactics. Davka, we'll go out and have a good time to prove to ourselves that we won't give him the satisfaction.

Too bad our Diaspora brethren don't see things the same way. Instead of rushing over to stand with us together to face the common enemy, they stay away in droves. The latest slap in the face was this week's decision of Reform leadership in the United States to cancel their summer youth trips here. The move precipitated condemnation from all quarters, including embarrassed Israeli Reform "machers." The decision brought a swift end to any residue of sympathy for the Reform movement's struggle for acceptance here.

While we do our best under trying circumstances to go on with life as usual and thumb our noses at Arafat, his Fatah and Tanzim, the Diaspora caves in and hands them all a victory of sorts. The half-empty planes and deserted hotels show how easy it's been to make a dent in the shield that used to unite the Jewish people.

Where in the World?

Jerusalem, July 15, 2001 Where in the world do 7,000 people turn out for the opening of one of the best international film festivals, filling the bleachers of an ancient garden to view a light-hearted satire on a huge screen under the stars? Where can you watch an exuberant fireworks display over the walls of one of the world's most venerable cities?

Where would you spend a leisurely Friday morning wandering in a quaint neighborhood choosing between an assortment of street-side cafes for your rendezvous with friends on this first day of the weekend? Where could you hear the lively sounds of Honduran street musicians playing to an appreciative, relaxed crowd in a little square near the center of town? Where do you wake up every morning to sunshine and bright bougainvillea?

Where do you have trouble choosing from the array of fine restaurants to suit every taste and level of kashrut? Where do you have difficulty figuring out how to listen to two or three world-class lecturers who happen to be speaking on the same evening? Where can you attend an international conference on any topic of Jewish interest almost every day of the week? Where do the world's most renowned rabbis and teachers give classes every night of the week?

Where do Jewish kids dance till the wee hours at discos all over the city? Where could you sit in on a radio show to listen to Bibi Netanyahu being interviewed in English? Where are some of the world's most precious Jewish artifacts housed? Where is there a zoo that identifies the animals of the Bible? Where could you go shopping in a cool, underground arcade used by shoppers thousands of years ago? Where do you make friends with Jews from every corner of the globe? Where could you witness the largest gathering of Jewish athletes in the world? The list could go on and on...

The only place in the world where all these things are happening is right here in the middle of the CNN/BBC/NPR-designated war zone. Jerusalem, capital of the Jewish state, just minutes away from where Jews are being attacked and murdered daily, is a vibrant center of Jewish cultural, social and educational life.

That's a message we need to convey to Jews abroad — come and enjoy the unique opportunities Jerusalem has to offer.

On the other hand, we citizens of the holy city must struggle with the fine line between going about our work and social/cultural lives even in the face of the mounting Jewish death toll and becoming too accustomed and even inured to the ghastly results of the Arab war against the Jews.

As the violence wears on towards its one-year anniversary, it looks like a reality we'll continue to face.

Remembering Entebbe
A Message for Today?

Jerusalem, July 3, 2001   Yes, we CAN do hasbara (PR for Israel)! That fact was proven tonight at the official state commemoration of the 25th anniversary of Operation Yonatan, the Entebbe rescue mission.

In a masterful, moving event that was both entertaining and educational, the State of Israel marked the passage of a quarter of a century since the dramatic rescue of 103 hostages from Entebbe, Uganda. If last night's event were to be translated and exported, Israel's image problems might be improved dramatically, and Jews the world over would begin to regain their pride in the Jewish state.

For the past week, the nation has focused on the unprecedented operation that took dozens of soldiers from Israel's elite brigades on a daring and dangerous mission to rescue Jews thousands of miles away.

The commander of the unit that undertook to carry out the plan was Yoni Netanyahu, older brother of former Prime Minister Binyamin Netanyahu. Yoni, who was thirty years old when he died, was the only soldier killed in the assault on the Ugandan airport.

The Netanyahu family home where Yoni, Bibi and Ido grew up is one block away from my apartment in the Old Katamon neighborhood of Jerusalem. The small square in front of the modest house where their father, Prof. Benzion Netanyahu, still lives, is named for Yoni, and Bibi's beige limo is a common sight there.

A few years after his death, the Netanyahu family published a book of Yoni's letters written over a 13-year period between 1963-1976. Entitled 'Self Portrait of a Hero,' the letters paint a picture of a passionate Zionist, as they chronicle Yoni's passage through the army and his participation as a paratrooper in two of the most crucial battles of the Six Day War.

Last week, a TV documentary focused on Yoni Netanyahu's career, featuring extensive photos, film clips and interviews with his brothers and former girlfriend. True to form, a columnist in the left-leaning Haaretz newspaper said the program, "seems more like a propaganda film," and opines "the Yoni that emerges from the film is not a flesh and blood character, but something closer to a modern day Bar Kochba."

Indeed, the old-fashioned Zionist values exemplified by Yoni and the Entebbe campaign put into sharp relief the thinking of post-Zionists who dominate the Israeli media and intellectual debate in this country.

Last night's event that took place at Jerusalem's Binyanei Haooma conference hall was attended by the nation's leading politicians; those who took part in the Entebbe operation — former hostages and their rescuers; and thousands of soldiers who serve today in Sayeret Matkal, Tzanchanim and Golani — the brigades that carried out the rescue 25 years ago.

On film, we watched as the political leaders of 1976 debated what to do about the Jewish hostages who had been sitting under Idi Amin's guard for days. The familiar faces of Yitzhak Rabin, Yigal Allon, Yitzhak Navon and Shimon Peres flitted across the screen.

Interspersed with the film clips, the accomplished singing troupes of several army and air force divisions belted out some of the old rousing Israeli anthems.

President Moshe Katzav, truly a man of the people, with modest and dignified demeanor, thanked those who had liberated the hostages on behalf of the state. "We say to the terrorists of today: We did it then and we can do it now if we want."

There are several minutes of footage of former hostages describing their ordeal. They tell of their disbelief that the IDF had sent their forces across the African continent to rescue them. In excruciating detail they calmly recount the selection procedure that separated the Jews and Israelis from the non-Jewish passengers on the Air France flight.

Foreign Minister Shimon Peres rose to speak without notes, and chose to address himself to the assembled young soldiers who filled the hall. He urged them not to think of the Entebbe fighters as legendary heroes. "Each of you has the potential to do the same thing," he said. "You represent the best hope for the people."

Next on film was a short clip of an interview with a handsome, middle aged civilian who was a pilot of one of the Hercules planes that left the Sirkin air force base for the seven hour trip to Entebbe. "We were so afraid of failure," he says, his dark eyes staring unflinchingly into the camera. "But on the way back, I felt like it was Pesach. I recalled the words of the Hagaddah: 'I and no angel: I and no messenger...brought you out of the land of Egypt,' concluded the pilot who wore no kippa on his silver hair. "If they told me now, 25 years later, to go on such a mission, I'd go without hesitation. Ayn Lanu Eretz Acheret — we have no other country," he said, in a theme that was to echo throughout the evening.

Film interviews with others involved in the rescue followed. Almost all those who played significant roles in Entebbe went on to illustrious military and political careers. We watched as Ehud Barak, Matan Vilnai, Dan Shomron and Ephraim Sneh spoke of their recollections 25 years on. Shomron, the overall planner of the operation, told the former hostages: "We knew we were endangering you too. No one had any idea how many would fall. You were part of the campaign, you're part of the fight against terror."

Two of the paratroopers came on stage to read short statements in their own words about their feelings on the anniversary of the operation. One tall, balding man with a gray mustache said he was disappointed that his teenage son's classmates knew nothing about Operation Yonatan. "We're facing the same things today — they need more than virtual Zionism," he said.

Benny, a younger man who was only 13 years old when he was

taken hostage by the terrorists, told the audience in a trembling voice that he remembers every moment of the torment. "I was a kid who saw death in front of him."

Tzipi Cohen was only eight years old when she witnessed her father, Pasco, bleeding to death, as he was accidentally shot by Israeli soldiers in the confusion of the rescue. Pasco Cohen raised his head to look for his son when the shooting started. He was one of four Jewish hostages who perished in Uganda. His daughter ended her brief remarks by reiterating her gratitude to the IDF for saving the hostages, despite her personal tragedy.

The final segment of the two hour program was entitled, 'The Price.' Besides the loss of Yoni Netanyahu and the four hostages, one soldier, Surin Hershko, became a paraplegic as a result of the injuries he sustained at Entebbe. We watched on screen as Surin used his computer at home. He uses an elongated straw manipulated by his mouth to write on the keyboard. Hershko is completely paralyzed, but rolled to the front of the auditorium in his wheelchair to reminisce about the last time he ran or walked. "I remember what it was to be a fighter," he recalled.

After presenting Hershko with a special medal commemorating Entebbe, Prime Minister Ariel Sharon delivered a speech that tied Israel's efforts to combat terror in the 1970s to today's struggle against the same enemy:

> In these confusing times, when there are those who question our capabilities or the justness of our cause, we return to those few hours when Israel stood up and in the face of the entire community of nations, waged a battle against violence and terrorism, proving that we can win.
>
> These days, when we are in the midst of an ongoing battle against terrorism, violence and incitement, and when we are making a joint national effort to return to political negotiations without fire, we must rekindle the spirit of that operation. The secret of our strength lies in such spirit and faith, and if we

learn how to renew it we will be able to meet all the challenges that still lie ahead.

The poignancy of the moment was overwhelming as rescuers and rescued mounted the stage to join the young IDF choir members in singing Hatikva as the evening drew to a close.

Tisha B'Av 5761

Jerusalem, July 29, 2001   Tisha B'Av 5761: The fast day commemorating the fall of the first and second Temples. Another day when the media distorted events here in Jerusalem and played into the hands of those bent on inflaming tensions.

A silent, dignified erev Tisha B'Av march by tens of thousands of Jews around the walls of the Old City was completely ignored by both Israeli and world media. The day after Tisha B'Av, the story was not the rocks hurled at Jewish worshipers standing in prayer at the Western Wall, but the reaction of Israeli forces who went up on the Temple Mount and managed to quell the riots in just a few minutes.

The traditional walk around the walls of the city attracted throngs of Israelis who gathered across from the US Consulate on Agron Street half an hour after Shabbat. Many of us were concerned that the turnout would be adversely affected because those living outside Jerusalem would have difficulty getting there so soon after Shabbat, or that the hazards on the roads would keep people from coming into the city. But even as the baal koreh (public reader) starts to chant the mournful Eicha (Lamentations) over the microphone, thousands cluster on the grass holding flashlights, straining to hear every word.

Across the street, the US flag flutters atop the consulate building, as wary consular security officials keep watch on the crowd. Just a little way up the block, the gaudy blue neon cross atop the French Catholic church shines out into the night.

As the marchers move off following a huge banner proclaiming our slogan of allegiance to Jerusalem, organizer Nadia Matar reminds the crowd that this is not a demonstration or a rally, nor is it a social event. In fact, no reminder is necessary, as the restrained mass of Jews soberly sets out to encircle the gates of the Holy City.

Scattered amongst the marchers are quite a number of non-observant people. Women wearing pants and sleeveless tops walk side by side with others whose hair is carefully covered with scarf or hat. Many parents are there with small children, as are large numbers of older people. Walking up the hill to Tzahal Square we turn to look back at those behind. People as far back as we can see — accompanied by huge Israeli flags, quietly taking part in an ancient Jerusalem tradition.

On down past New Gate, traffic traveling in the opposite direction on Route #1 is held up as we take over the streets and pour down the road toward Damascus Gate. Most of the Arab stores are shuttered tight, but a 24-hour bakery is open, its few customers studiously ignoring our presence. A few shebab (Arab youth) are loitering around Herod's Gate, accompanied by the ubiquitous Israeli police burdened on this warm night by bullet-proof vests.

In front of us we see the Mount of Olives crowned with its Arab and Christian institutions. Despite its Jewish historic and spiritual

"Turning the corner to walk along the eastern wall of the Old City, we take in a breathtaking view of the world's oldest Jewish cemetery on the Mt. of Olives."

significance, the only living Jewish presence on the Mount today is Beit Orot, the hesder yeshiva and development initiative.

Turning the corner to walk along the eastern wall, we look out at the vast expanse of the oldest Jewish cemetery in the world. Sticking out like a sore thumb is the Ras el Amud mosque built on the southeastern corner of the cemetery. The green neon illuminating the tower is mysteriously extinguished as we come to a halt in front of Lion's Gate — the gate used by the paratroopers who liberated the Old City in 1967.

As a few Arab kids play noisily in a house above, we listen in silence to the words of Temple Mount archeologist Gabi Barkai, Rabbi Moti Elon and Rabbi Shalom Gold. "They tell us that approaching Har Habyit (The Temple Mount) is dangerous these days," said Rabbi Elon. "I say turning our backs on Har Habayit is what's dangerous."

Many of us wander over to the wall to gaze at Absalom's Tomb and the monument to the prophet Zecharia in the Kidron Valley below. Across the valley we can see the new Maale Hazeitim development that acts as a buffer between Abu Dis, home of Arafat's parliament building, and the Temple Mount. Rounding the corner, we look up at the imposing Southern Wall of the Temple with the steps and the Huldah Gate, before making the ascent towards Dung Gate and the entrance to the Western Wall. Glancing backwards again, the sight of the masses of people still behind us is awesome. Quiet and dignified, the march has gone off without incident.

Tisha B'Av morning the media were already full of screaming headlines about Arab reaction to the annual effort by members of the Temple Mount Faithful to go up to the Temple Mount. The group generally attracts only 30 people, and Israel's High Court had already ruled last week that the Faithful would not be permitted to carry out a cornerstone laying ceremony on the site. Israeli police had given assurances that no such action would be tolerated.

Nevertheless, the usual Arab spokesmen still call the the group a provocation and threaten that they won't be able to control the ensuing violence. As if on cue, at around 11 a.m. rocks are hurled from above onto Jewish worshipers in the Western Wall plaza below. People start running for cover, some using plastic chairs as protection against the barrage. Within moments, hundreds of Israeli police in riot gear run through the gate atop Robinson's Arch and onto the Temple Mount. All it takes is about three minutes to subdue the agitators. But the headlines had already been written. "Israeli troops storm Moslem holy site," trumpets one wire service.

The morning's events impact another traditional Tisha B'av observance. Later in the afternoon, when calm is restored, Rav Ariel makes an announcement to a few hundred people gathered to observe the custom of reciting prayers and blowing silver trumpets at the gates of the Temple Mount. Due to security concerns, the police prohibit the group from carrying out their annual observance. We will have to make do with a token ritual at the top of the stairs looking over the Mount and then down below at Robinson's Arch. The planned mincha (afternoon service) that was to have taken place at the Huldah Gate is cancelled.

Reviving the ancient tradition of encircling the walls of Jerusalem, sounding the trumpet at the gates of the Temple Mount.

Instead, a few of us head to the Kotel Hakatan, the small section of the Wall closest to the Holy of Holies. In the cool tunnel on the way to the Moslem Quarter, a few men are stretched out to rest. One is dressed in sackcloth, the traditional mourning dress.

The alleyways to the Kotel Hakatan are heavily guarded, but all is calm at the tiny courtyard of the Wall. Rabbanit Chana Henkin, dean of Nishmat, is davening (praying) there with a few other women. As we prepare to leave, we're replaced by a contingent of yeshiva students from Beit El.

Back in the plaza of the Western Wall, the tired, hot and hungry are sprawled on the ground waiting for the fast to be over. A thirty-something policewoman in pants is downing a bottle of water. Apologetically she announces to her friend that she's still fasting, and is taking only water to be able to work.

So forget about what you've seen on CNN or heard on NBC, CBS or the BBC. The Jews have once again taken seriously the observance of Tisha B'Av, even if it means enduring rocks and a bad press.

Europeans in the Middle East: Assistance or Interference?

Jerusalem, August 25, 2001   After the Tel Aviv disco attack that claimed twenty-one young Israeli lives, German foreign minister Joschka Fischer, who was in the area at the time, reportedly threatened to sever European Union (EU) relations with Yasser Arafat if the Palestinian leader did not clamp down on terror.

Fischer's words of rebuke ring a little hollow, given the reality of EU activity in the Middle East.

In coordination with the Palestinians, but without Israeli approval, a group of European "security coordinators" turned up last May in Beit Jala, just outside Jerusalem. EU foreign policy chief Javier Solana tried to brush off the presence of the small force, calling it a technical team to advise the Palestinians on how to implement the ceasefire. But EU-Israeli tensions were raised when Prime Minister Ariel Sharon angrily complained about the observers to the visiting then EU president, Swedish Prime Minister Goeran Persson. The EU crew is widely seen to be the vanguard of a de facto international force — something Israel has long opposed.

The question of where the EU directs its Middle East funding is probably an even better indicator of European intentions in the region.

EU money not only directly supports the Palestine Authority (PA) through its three billion dollar financial aid package directed straight into PA coffers, but the Europeans are also the major backers of dozens of projects sponsored by Palestinian and Jewish organizations dedicated to "ending the occupation" or influencing public opinion against the policies of the Sharon government.

According to Jean Breteche, European Commission representative to the West Bank and Gaza, the EU's mandate in the area is "to instill humanitarian principles, respect for human rights and the concept of a viable democracy." Breteche asserts that the Europeans are primarily committed to "health and education" projects.

Even a cursory reading of a 1999 European Commission report on projects funded by its People to People initiative makes it clear that the EU agenda is, in fact, far from humanitarian in nature.

Take the Middle East Center for Legal and Economic Research (MEILER), for example. MEILER received 300,000 Euro ($280,000) in 1999 from the EU to conduct phase two of a survey of Palestinian Refugee Real Estate Holdings in Israel. Working from Orient House, the PA's Jerusalem headquarters, MEILER assists Arabs living in refugee camps to research property in 531 Arab villages abandoned in 1948.

The exercise is not merely theoretical. Orient House employees acknowledge that the information is to be used by Arabs to claim compensation as well as land.

EU largesse is also directed at influencing public opinion in Europe regarding contentious land issues. A new recipient of EU funding is a joint project between two non-profit Palestinian organizations, the Applied Research Institute (ARIJ) and the Land Research Center (LRC).

This effort, in the words of ARIJ, "aims at inspecting and scrutinizing Israeli colonizing activities in their different forms" and to "disseminate the related information to policy makers in the European countries and to the general public."

Courtesy of the EU, these groups, who liberally scatter the word "colonies" throughout their materials, plan to use remote sensing satellite images and aerial photographs to monitor Israeli construction activity.

The International Committee on House Demolitions (ICAHD) is another patently political recipient of EU support. The group's mission statement explains that ICAHD activities are designed to "resist all aspects of the Occupation," and to "initiate legal challenges to Israeli actions and policies in the Occupied Territories."

Organizations such as ICAHD wouldn't exist if it were not for the generosity of the EU. In 1999, the annual ICAHD budget was 385,000 Euro. The European Commission granted the group 250,000 (approx. $222,000) or 65 percent of the total. On a recent lecture tour in the United States, ICAHD director Jeff Halper reportedly equated Israel's legal system with the Nazi Nuremberg Laws.

Legal efforts against Jewish development in eastern Jerusalem were also financed by EU money. The EU funded 100% of the 1999 budget of Ir Shalem, providing the group the backing to litigate against Israeli purchase of former Jewish homes in the Moslem Quarter and development of the Har Homa, Beit Orot and Ras el Amud neighborhoods.

In more blatant disregard for its governing humanitarian principles, the EU has directed some of its largest contributions to several programs that attempt to persuade the large voting bloc of immigrants from the former Soviet Union to reverse its traditional conservative voting pattern.

Peace Now received 400,000 Euro (approx. $340,000) to implement an outreach program to the immigrants. In addition, a separate grant of the same amount was allocated to an institute led by Knesset member Roman Bronfman. The Institute for Democracy and Leadership Training ran a "peace and democracy awareness campaign," with the explicit goal stated in the grant application, to bring "Russian immigrants in Israel into the peace camp."

Another 350,000 Euro grant was recently approved to fund the activities of Teena, a Jerusalem-based non-profit group. With its EU money, Teena will organize activities in Russian on various aspects of the Arab world. The principal objective of the effort is "to change public opinion within the community in favor of peace settlement based on territorial compromise and mutual concessions."

Through the language of its own communiqués, one may gauge

the EU's disposition toward Israel. In a January 18, 2001, press release about a new grant, the EU Commission Representation tacked on a final paragraph denouncing "excessive and dispropor- tionate use of force by the State of Israel against Palestinian civilians," without so much as a mention of Palestinian terror attacks against Israeli Jews.

After the Yom Kippur War EU member nations supplied arms to hostile Arab nations. Today, European nations fund school textbooks used by the Palestinian Authority that promote hatred of Jews and intolerance of Israel's right to exist.

Under the guise of promoting peace and democracy, the EU in fact abuses Israeli openness and undermines its democracy through its grants to groups that operate outside the national consensus.

Europeans, with their not-so-distant dismal colonial history and the collaboration of many of their governments during WWII, have no credentials to operate in the Mid-East tinderbox. Perhaps their pro-Palestinian bias is an outgrowth of mass Moslem immigration with which many European nations are now trying to cope. In Belgium, seat of the current EU rotating presidency, 10 percent of the population is now Moslem. (Jews number 80,000.)

But whatever the reason, the escalation of EU involvement in the region through funding, personnel on the ground and subvention of NGO initiatives makes it clear that it's not assistance but interference Europe is delivering to the Middle East.

Welcome To Israel

Jerusalem, September 12, 2001   After every terrorist attack in Israel, concerned Americans call to check up on their friends and relatives in Jerusalem. Yesterday, the tables were turned as horrified Israelis watched from afar the unfolding American tragedy of almost unfathomable proportions. This time it was we who feared for the safety of our loved ones living in Washington and New York.

The frantic calls to check on relatives; the race to tune into any available news source; the stunned disbelief as lives are altered in a chilling instant. Here in Israel, where we have become so familiar with the macabre routine of the post-terror minutes and hours, it's almost unbearable to watch as tens of thousands of Americans have been made to suffer the same agony.

Unlike in America, however, where Starbucks shuttered all their facilities, and shopping malls and office buildings all over the country were closed to the public, the Israeli response to terror is to act with resolve. Streets are cleaned immediately, and it's a return to business as usual as quickly as possible. Every bombing or drive-by shooting reinforces the national sense of unity and purpose — precisely the opposite reaction the terrorists hope to evoke.

Over the past year of intensified attacks against Jewish civilians, many Israelis felt that the world did not fully comprehend the extent of base hatred that motivated young Arabs to blow themselves up in shopping malls and train stations, outside discos or in pizza parlors. Why couldn't we explain that, while we stand on the front line of the fight against radical Islamic fundamentalism, the US and Western values are the larger target?

As the Western media labeled the perpetrators of attacks against schoolteachers and infants as "activists" or "guerillas," we shook our heads in disbelief. As the US and Israeli flags burned together at violent protests in Ramallah and Nablus, we wondered who was paying attention. As US State Department officials criticized Israel's policy of targeted killings of known terrorist leaders, we didn't understand why the rest of the civilized world wasn't marveling at the precision of our military intelligence in taking out terrorist thugs with minimal loss of civilian life.

And we couldn't comprehend how world leaders could call on Prime Minister Arik Sharon to exercise "restraint" in the face of the mounting death toll.

Yesterday, as Israelis learned of the tragedy unfolding in America's power centers, a solidarity demonstration took place spontaneously outside the US Embassy in Tel Aviv. The defense minister ordered our special IDF disaster evacuation unit to fly to the US, and a call for blood donors was answered by hundreds of citizens.

Meanwhile, our Arab neighbors were handing out candies and dancing on Sultan Suleiman Street in eastern Jerusalem and in Nablus as they heard the news.

Their reaction had little to do with Israeli "settlements" or the "occupation." Those who took the lives of so many Americans yesterday, and those who sympathize with them, no longer have a cover for their intolerance and hatred of Christians and Jews. Yesterday they took off the mask. Is the world really looking?

KGB: Thanks For the Memories

Jerusalem, December 5, 2001   It's a bitterly cold Moscow morning in December 1985. Refusenik Natasha Khassina is home caring for her eight year old daughter who's sick. Khassina wears a worn housecoat and a weary smile. A modest headscarf covers her dark brown hair in the universal style of Orthodox women.

I listen as Khassina goes through the motions of describing to her American visitors the dreadful limbo condition endured by her family after years of refusal in their quest to emigrate to Israel.

Fast-forward sixteen years and half a world away to a Saturday night in December at Darna, one of Jerusalem's more expensive restaurants. Khassina strides in to meet visiting congressman Mark Kirk (R-Il) along with a group of her fellow former Jewish activists.

The round face and high cheekbones are still there. But Khassina, the Israeli, is now dressed in a fashionable pantsuit, her hair stylishly cropped.

I fumble in my bag to fish out a slightly faded photo of our 1985 visit. Khassina laughs at the images of us both 16 years younger, but says nothing about her transformation.

Kirk has requested the meeting with former prisoners of Zion and refuseniks to cap his first visit to Israel as an elected official. The youthful looking, trim congressman served for many years as foreign policy aide to Rep. John Porter, known to all those present as one of the strongest congressional voices on behalf of Soviet Jews.

The men sitting around the table had all spent time in Soviet jails or labor camps for their "anti-Soviet" activities. Ephraim Kholmiansky was arrested for teaching Hebrew; Yevgeny Lein spent a year in Siberia for his Jewish activities; Ari Volvovsky, another Hebrew teacher, had run afoul of the KGB, and Yosef Mendelevich was a key player in a desperate plan to gain freedom that involved hijacking a twelve-seater plane to Sweden, returning the aircraft to the Soviet Union, and making their escape to Israel. The group was caught before they even stepped foot on the plane, and the ensuing show trial, culminating in death sentences for two participants, was the impetus for western Jewry to take up the cause of oppressed Soviet Jews.

Natasha Khassina was the only one amongst the crowd who was never arrested for her Jewish activities. During her years as a refusenik in Moscow, she was known as one of the boldest activists, going about her Hebrew lessons and efforts to organize women refuseniks quite openly.

All of the former refuseniks and prisoners have rebuilt their lives in Israel. Natasha and husband Gennady are residents of Gilo. The Leins live in the Jerusalem suburb of Maale Adumim, with their two children and six grandchildren nearby. Kholmiansky, Volvovsky and Mendelevich are all Torah observant and involved with absorption efforts. The Volvovskys have lived in the Gush Etzion community of Efrat since they arrived in Israel some 14 years ago.

Mendelevich, twenty-three years old at the time he was sentenced for the hijack attempt, emerged from Chistopol prison 11 years later and arrived in Israel to a tumultuous welcome. Tonight, this fifty-four year old with wispy, long gray beard and steely eyes is persuaded to recount his story to the visiting congressman.

And then Congressman Kirk drops the best line of the evening: "So, I guess I'm going to recommend you to the FAA as the new US airport security consultant!"

In a more serious vein, Mendelevich thanks the congressman for American support of the Soviet Jewry movement. "You gave significant help to the Jewish liberation movement when we were still in the FSU," he says. But he won't let Kirk get away without telling him in forceful terms the kind of help he feels the Jewish people needs now. "Today we feel as if we're in the midst of the struggle for our homeland. The Arabs never admit that we have the right to stay here. I ask you today, not to allow them to deceive world opinion."

Lein, a secular Jew from Maale Adumim who had stood up to the KGB at his Leningrad trial, adds: "You have to realize that we are those who fought to be here. We won't accept that our enemies are trying to force us out. I'm proud that my son served in the IDF. We need all your help to tell President Bush not to trust Yasser Arafat."

Outside in the cool Jerusalem evening, we go our separate ways. The Kirk party heads back to its hotel for a few hours sleep before returning to Chicago and Washington. The Volvovskys drive off to Efrat via the tunnel road that they find closed for the first time in a few weeks, due to the resumption of Arabs shooting at Gilo. Natasha leaves for her home in Gilo and a night punctured by gunfire. Yevgeny and the Kholmianskys take the bus back to Maale Adumim, east of the city, along a road that has seen sporadic attacks in recent months.

The context may have changed, but the players — passionate activists and sympathetic elected officials — and the struggle itself, go on.

Rep. Mark Kirk (left) examines a copy of Yevgeny Lein's lifestory as the former Prisoner of Zion looks on.

In the Shadow of Death

Jerusalem, December 2, 2001   After a week when funeral followed funeral, last night's terror attack on the youth of Jerusalem was too much to take.

Everyone knows that it's the kids who are out in the cafes of downtown Jerusalem at 11:30 p.m. on a Saturday night. The corner of Ben Yehuda Street where the first two explosions pierced the night was home to a popular ice cream store and a dairy restaurant under strict mehadrin kashrut supervision. The terrorist maniacs blew themselves up in the midst of groups of young people out to celebrate a birthday party. What kind of political statement is that?

This morning's newspaper headlines said it all: "The whole country is terror," writes Yediot columnist Roni Shaked. Chaim Shibi's column runs under the heading: "Life in the shadow of death." Indeed, it's becoming increasingly difficult not to feel that we're all living under that shadow.

At home in Old Katamon last night, the sounds of terror penetrated the windows shuttered against the cold of a December evening. First, at around 11 p.m., the now familiar dull thuds of shelling and return fire could be heard from the direction of Gilo. Not forty-five minutes later, the wailing sirens of scores of ambulances broke in to the north and east of the neighborhood. Soon, the phone started ringing with calls from friends and family in the States who heard about the horror just as Shabbat was ending in New York.

Local and international TV crews broadcast live from the Ben Yehuda scene, a mere 10 minutes away. Watching the third detonation, a car filled with explosives and mortar shells, turn Rav Kook Street into a fireball, it was hard not to recall the images of New York on September 11. Rescue workers could be seen running for their lives up Jaffa Road as the fireball engulfed the side street.

Dark smoke billowed up into the sky from the small street lined with historic buildings.

The TV coverage went on into the night, but my alarm was set for 4:45 a.m. to take a visiting friend to the airport for an early morning flight back to the States. Neither of us needed the alarm, however, as the evening's images were not conducive to sleep. Driving through the deserted Jerusalem streets and along the quiet Jerusalem-Tel Aviv highway, we made it to the airport in little more than half an hour.

Instead of turning around and heading home to mournful Jerusalem, I decide to go on to Tel Aviv for a walk on the beach to try to erase some of the images of the night. The full moon still shines in the sky over the Mediterranean as the winter waves lap the soft sand. A few lone walkers and runners stride close to the shore, paying little attention to the hardy, older Russians who may be seen taking their morning swim in the bracing water.

Planes bank low overhead, flying in and out of nearby Ben Gurion airport, as if all were normal. But today, Israel is far from normal. Walking south on the beach, it's impossible to avoid the Dolphinarium. Once a lively nightspot, all that remains is a triangular stone memorial at the site where 21 young revelers lost their lives six short months ago. The motto inscribed on the stone in English, Hebrew and Russian could just as well be read as an epitaph for last night's victims in Jerusalem. "In memory of innocent citizens. Among them many youngsters whose lives were cut off by murderers in a bloody terror attack on Friday night, June 1, 2001. May they rest in peace." Fresh flowers and wreaths adorn the site where the victim's families and survivors gather every Friday morning for mutual support.

Just across the street to the north is the anonymous grey concrete building housing the American embassy. Security guards lounge on the white trucks strategically parked to block the entrances. A new guardhouse is under construction to further scrutinize incoming visitors.

All along the beach, people go about their morning tasks listlessly, laboring under the shadow of the endless parade of death. The owner of one of the cafe/bars that sits on the sand looking out over the sea pulls tables and chairs out from under their overnight cover and stares distractedly off into the horizon. As the sun rises over the city to the east, casting a warm hue over the water, there's none of the lively anticipation of another beautiful day at the beach that would accompany a cafe proprietor in Miami Beach.

As the traffic starts to build, I leave the beach in search of one of the new Starbucks cafes opened in Tel Aviv a few weeks ago. I find it across the street from another painful site. It's at 70 Ibn Gvirol Street. The outdoor tables look out at the spot on Kikar Rabin where Yitzhak Rabin was assassinated in 1995. Inside, the few patrons who can afford a $3 cup of coffee are exchanging comments on the Jerusalem tragedy.

Driving back to Jerusalem, I can't resist turning on the radio for the news. I'm holding my breath waiting for the names of last night's victims to be announced. Instead, there's a bulletin about another attack near the southern community of Alei Sinai. One man is dead, several injured. This is where a young couple was murdered two months ago when terrorists broke into the village and went on a killing rampage. The father of one of the youngsters, Liron Harpaz, is interviewed. I'm listening to his pained words just as we pass the Har Hamenuchot cemetery at the outskirts of Jerusalem, where fresh graves are being prepared for last night's victims.

The radio anchor reads off a few of the faxes listeners have sent in. They all voice similar sentiments: Let the IDF get on with it. We've had enough.

I can't help thinking about a pamphlet I read over Shabbat. It was found in a second hand bookstore here by a friend. It's a small item published in 1919 by the Central Office of the Zionist Organization in England, entitled: A Report on the Pogroms in Poland. In its 36 pages the author describes in detail, community by community, the extent of the pogroms that spread across Galicia in 1918.

Synagogues defiled, women raped, Jews murdered. A Jewish Self-Defense Corps of one thousand men was formed, the author notes, but they were quickly disarmed and disbanded by the Polish military authorities, leaving millions of Jews defenseless against the base hatred of their neighbors.

How much have we progressed, I wonder? Today we have a Jewish army, reputed to be one of the best in the world, yet its hands seem to be tied, and it is rendered powerless to protect the citizens it is charged to defend. I'm sure the Zionist Organization of 1919 could never have imagined such a scenario — Jews being murdered in the Jewish state because they are Jews, despite the presence of a strong Jewish army. Everyone acknowledges the large number of attacks that have been foiled by good IDF, police and intelligence work, but the specter of Jewish power restrained as the daily murder toll climbs is still too much to bear.

Arriving home, there are more calls to make to friends to find out if everyone's OK. The next radio bulletin: another bus bomb in Haifa. At least 16 dead, 40 injured this time, 17 in critical condition.

Now the names of the victims of the Jerusalem attack are released:

- Yuri Kurganov, 20 years old.
- Yosef Elezra, 18 years old.
- Moshe Yedid Levy, 19 years old.
- Golan Tourjeman, 15 years old.
- Assaf Avitan, 15 years old.
- Nir Heftzdi, 19 years old.
- Michael Moshe Dahan, 20 years old.
- Adam Weinstein, 14 years old.
- Guy Vaknin, 19 years old.
- Yisrael Yakov Danino, 17 years old.

May their memories be for a blessing. The friends who watched them die will live forever under the shadow of death.

One Week After

Jerusalem, December 8, 2001   Last Saturday night, yeshiva student Netanel Miller,18, lay in a Jerusalem hospital with shrapnel in his leg. Today, Miller's apartment is full of his young friends who came to celebrate Shabbat with the fortunate survivor of the Ben Yehuda terror attack. They came to sing, and to rejoice that their friend is home and alive.

Netanel, my neighbor, was released from the hospital earlier in the week, and has been hobbling around on crutches ever since. His answer to anyone who inquires after his health is "Baruch Hashem," Thank God.

Tonight, after Shabbat, the scene at the Ben Yehuda mall could not be more different from that one week ago. There are few people about. An air of quiet sadness hangs in the air. The main center of activity is the frantic preparation going on to ready the renovated plaza in Zion Square at the bottom of the mall for tomorrow's Chanukah candle lighting ceremony. Guests of honor will be New York Mayor Rudy Giuliani and New York Governor George Pataki.

There are pairs of soldiers every ten yards throughout the downtown area. Stores whose windows were blown out last Saturday evening are open for business tonight. The cell-phone store that was destroyed reopened on Tuesday. The young clerk working there now tells me she doesn't feel anything anymore. "I ignore everything," she says, as she recounts how she'd closed the store last Saturday night twenty minutes before the bombs ripped through the ice cream shop across the way.

There are two memorials set up on the mall to the boys who died there. Both have lit candles, flowers and notes set on them. A prayer shawl belonging to one victim is draped over one corner. Passers-by stop to say a quiet prayer, then move on.

A few people sit in Cafe Rimon, where one of the explosions

213

went off. Some kids sit defiantly at the ice cream store, too. Burger King, normally full of kids enjoying a kosher Saturday night treat, has a lone customer. The owner of one store can be seen painting over the patches where shrapnel has been removed. Police SWAT teams in their trademark black uniforms drive up and down the mall on motorcycles.

At around 8:45 pm a group of people from a Nachlaot synagogue gathers to begin a memorial service. They're led by the young, US born, rabbi of Shir Hadash, Ian Pear. Rav Ian and his wife Rachel are building a vibrant, young community around them in the central Jerusalem neighborhood that's just up the street from Ben Yehuda. Tonight, in front of cameras from CNN and several Israeli and foreign stations, Rav Ian speaks about the importance of remembrance. He reminds those present that our victims are all innocent children who were enjoying a night out. He pointedly notes that Palestinian casualties are almost always struck down while committing acts of violence.

As he speaks, a distraught young man with tears in his eyes and slicked back hair approaches and whispers in his ear. He tells Rav Ian that his friend, Ido Cohen, 17, one of those injured last week, has just died in the hospital. Pushing his way back through the crowd, the leather clad boy sobs that he's on his way to the funeral.

The havdala band that has created a Saturday night tradition in Kikar Tzion begins to play the soulful Carlebach tune, "Nachamu, Nachamu Ami." Be comforted my people.

Coping with the Lull

Jerusalem, December 20, 2001   In the lull between terror attacks (the question is not IF there will be another, but WHEN), Israel is struggling to cope with its domestic concerns.

Unfortunately for some members of the Knesset, the lull has coincided with budget talks. The recent spate of grisly Arab terror had eclipsed any other news for weeks, but now we're forced to deal with the economic and social disasters that continue to plague this country.

Unemployment figures just announced tell some of the story. Almost 10 percent of the workforce is currently unemployed — the highest number recorded since the establishment of the state. Since April there's been a steady 0.1 percent increase every month.

Not that we need the statistics to tell us. All of us know people who have been recently laid off, or are fearful of the fall of the next outsource ax. I have friends who are attorneys, high tech marketing managers, transportation engineers and office managers who are currently unemployed. This round of cutbacks has hit all sectors, not just blue-collar workers.

Meantime, strikes are breaking out all over to protest the proposed budget cuts. Today it's the turn of the Negev towns. Workers in Beersheva, Dimona, Kiryat Gat and Ofakim are closing down their towns today to let the government know what they think of the repeal of the Negev Law that granted special tax breaks to residents of the Negev.

Yesterday, a group of vocal, physically challenged Israelis broke into the Labor and Social Affairs Ministry, staging a sit-in in their wheelchairs to demand that their monthly allocations rise to the level of the minimum wage.

But poor Finance Minister Silvan Shalom has to find some way to cut 6.15 billion shekel from the 2002 budget. A good place to start would be some of the superfluous ministries that employ ministers, deputy ministers and an entire workforce of pekidim (clerks) all trying to look busy as they wait to reach retirement age and a cushy pension.

Even US Ambassador Daniel Kurtzer is getting in on the act with budget advice. Speaking at the annual meeting of the Israeli Center for Management yesterday, Kurtzer told the group that Israel cannot live with a budget deficit of 4 percent of GDP, which could occur if budget cuts are not made. He pleaded with the government to increase allocations to Arabs, Bedouin and development towns.

The one bright spot this week has been the weather. Precisely because it's not been bright and sunny. Rain has deluged the entire country, adding a few precious millimeters to the severely depleted Kinneret, Israel's main reservoir. We're still more than 180 centimeters below the red line, but this season has a distinctly more winter-like feel than winters past. There's snow on Mt. Hermon and the prospect of a real ski season up there.

For me, a former Londoner and Seattleite, the cool, damp is comfortingly familiar. Back in the old country, a highlight of my day was a brisk half hour walk around a traffic-free park on a peninsula sticking out into Lake Washington. Here in Jerusalem it's been difficult to duplicate the empty, tree-lined footpath with calm lake water lapping to one side. But a rainy morning stroll through Jerusalem neighborhoods has other compensations. It's far more interesting!

Today, even though it's not so cold, (around 10 degrees Centigrade) some of my neighbors are decked out as if they're facing a Toronto winter. Down parkas, boots, gloves and umbrellas are de rigueur. Every conversation along the street starts with a comment about the cold. In the San Simon Park I pass two Arab gardeners bundled up in sweaters, scarves and wool hats, their fingers wrapped around glasses of hot Turkish coffee.

On a nearby street, men carrying their tallit (prayer shawl) bags encased in protective plastic hurry in and out of the Shtiyblach. The

Shtiyblach is a unique synagogue where men can find a minyan (prayer quorum) forming every fifteen minutes around the clock. As I pass by, a loud argument breaks out between a resident of an adjacent apartment building and a synagogue latecomer who's trying to park his car on the pavement to dash in for morning prayers.

Back on the main street, a traffic jam forms as a "suspicious object" alert has caused police sappers to clear the road. This is a routine occurrence in all Jerusalem neighborhoods, as alert residents do not hesitate to call police if they see anything remotely suspicious. After the object is harmlessly reeled in to the police van, pedestrians and cars resume their rush hour frenzy.

The rain continues to pour down, so I duck into the supermarket, just managing to avoid bumping into an old woman loaded down with groceries. She emerges into the deluge wearing nothing more than a sweater and cotton skirt, and I realize that not everyone can afford to buy a winter wardrobe for the relatively short cold, wet season.

The lady at the cheese counter, who is generally upbeat and chatty, greets me with a sigh and a comment about our terrible economic circumstances. My next stop is the cafe next door where the smell of fresh croissants wafting out of the door makes it impossible to pass by. There, over a passable latte and one of those delectable croissants (yes, I know, the goal of the brisk walk was just completely negated), I run into a French immigrant I know from my ulpan days. He tells me about the frightening rise in anti-Semitic incidents in his former homeland and the increasing acceptance in polite society of overt expressions of anti-Jewish sentiment. I'm hearing the same thing from British friends, where the French ambassador to London just triggered an international incident by announcing at a dinner party that the current troubles in the world were caused by "that shitty little country Israel."

Still, all these troubles are infinitely preferable to the news of the murder of innocent Israelis we've become almost numbed to over the past few weeks. Scores of attacks against Jews have occurred since Arafat's speech disavowing terrorism last Sunday. Mercifully, none of them has resulted in death, and thus the incidents go largely unreported to all but the most inveterate Israel Internet news junkies.

So, we'll enjoy the lull while it lasts, and no doubt look back longingly at the domestic turmoil when the next bomb explodes.

GLOSSARY FOR JERUSALEM DIARIES

Aliya — immigration to Israel. Literally "going up" to Israel.

Am Yisrael — the people of Israel, the Jewish people.

Beit Hamikdash — the Holy Temple in Jerusalem.

Halakha — Jewish law.

Har Habayit — the Temple Mount.

Hesder yeshiva — institute of higher learning for men, where Jewish studies are combined with service in the Israel Defense Forces.

IDF — Israel Defense Forces.

Kever — burial place.

Kipa/kippot (pl) — head covering worn by observant Jewish men.

Knesset — Israel's parliament.

Kotel — Western Wall.

Magen David — shield of David symbol.

Meretz — left of center political party.

Minyan — quorum of ten men required for certain prayers.

Oneg Shabbat — Friday night gathering of song, speeches and light refreshments.

Pesuch — Passover.

Rabbanit — Learned woman teacher, generally wife of a rabbi.

Rosh Hashanah — Jewish New Year

Sabra — native born Israeli.

Shabbat — Sabbath.

Shas — predominantly Sephardic religious political party.

Shavuot — festival of weeks, celebrated seven weeks after Passover.

Shiva — seven day mourning period.

Shofar — ram's horn sounded on Jewish high holydays, on triumphal occasions, and as a wake up call to the people.

Tallit — prayer shawl.

Yahrzeit — Hebrew anniversary of death of an individual.

YESHA — acronym for Judea, Samaria and Gaza.

Yeshiva — institute of higher Jewish learning.

Yishuv — small Jewish community.

Yom Kippur — Day of Atonement.

PRAISE FOR 'JERUSALEM DIARIES'

"Thanks for sending the book. It is excellent."
John Rothmann, talk show host, KGO Radio, San Francisco

"I was deeply moved by Judy Lash Balint's reflections on her visit to the family of Vadim Norzhich. That two innocent reserve soldiers were brutally lynched, while the entire world looked on, is shocking just as news. The tragedy becomes personal, however, when we read about the victim and the family who mourns him. Ms. Balint's article helped to make Vadim more than the lifeless body we saw thrown from the second-story window of the Ramallah police station."
Debbie Berliner, Fortuna, CA

"I liked both your pieces very much. You have a very nice touch "
Jonathan Rosenblum, Jerusalem Post columnist

"I love your feisty, informed, unabashed opinions. Too rare among women."
Rochelle Distelheim, author, Chicago, IL

"After I read your latest piece about what it felt like to go get your gas mask, it occurred to me that there is a difference between you and most everyone else who makes aliyah. You all no doubt have similar experiences. You, however, know how to write about them. Your "slice of life" accounts of making aliyah possess the rare quality of being able to simultaneously stimulate the intellect, spark the imagination and push all sorts of emotional buttons. They crackle with clarity and truth."
Kent Swigard, Seattle, WA

"Your writing is beautiful and uplifting. Thank you!"
Dr. Miriam Adahan, Jerusalem

"Judy, thank you for writing this wonderful article ("The Spirit of the People"). It touched my heart and brought me hope."
Uziel Weingarten, Los Angeles, CA

"Your work is SO GOOD! You write beautifully and movingly."

Susan Rosenbluth, editor, The Jewish Voice, Englewood, NJ

"I'm just letting you know that your writings touch my heart and the hearts of all who read them. I make copies and give them to my staff at school regularly. They become the lead into our daily tehillim (Psalms). I'm sorry that there has been so much to write about lately. I wish it were quieter. May you continue to give us words of inspiration and help us to see the picture clearly."

Aviva Yablok, Teaneck, NJ

"I love the way you write. It's so real and immediate. I feel as though I was there with you."

Helen Freedman, New York

"I do get tired of email, but I never tire of reading yours. Your words go right to my mind in visions that help me understand and remember."

Rabbi David S. Levin, Queens, NY

"I *loved* your story! Who needs television when you have that?"

Kevin Roddy, Hawaii

"Your articles are moving and powerful. I send them to everyone I know. They touch all who read them. They inspire the activists and push the observer into action."

Hillary Markowitz, Westchester, NY

"I really enjoyed your articles. You write so beautifully. They are very powerful, tear-provoking."

Chaya Siegelbaum, Seattle, WA

"Her diaries make me want to hop on the next plane, they are so visually rich."

Maxine Elkins, Philadelphia, PA

"Judy Lash Balint is simply an outstanding writer. She has total understanding of where she is and how to express it."

Dr. Alon Mintz, Israel